FORMOSA
under Chinese
Nationalist Rule

FORMOSA
under Chinese Nationalist Rule

FRED W. RIGGS

1972
OCTAGON BOOKS
New York

Reprinted 1972

by special arrangement with Fred W. Riggs

OCTAGON BOOKS

A DIVISION OF FARRAR, STRAUS & GIROUX, INC.

19 Union Square West

New York, N. Y. 10003

LIBRARY OF CONGRESS CATALOG CARD NUMBER: 76-38816

ISBN 0-374-96807-1

Manufactured by Braun-Brumfield, Inc.
Ann Arbor, Michigan

Printed in the United States of America

Preface

After forty years as a little known Japanese colony the island of Formosa has in recent years become a major focus of Far Eastern international diplomacy and strategy. It has also become a central issue in a long and bitter political wrangle over what should be American policy toward an aggressive Communist-controlled China. Ever since President Truman's dramatic decision in 1950 to "insulate" Formosa from the mainland, public attention has been directed to the island primarily as a stake and a symbol in international politics. Hence discussions about Formosa have often been conducted in symbolic terms. It has been variously described as a bastion against Chinese Communist imperialism, as a showcase for democracy, as the last citadel of Kuomintang reaction, as a vital point in America's Far Eastern defense line, and in similar picturesque but often exaggerated terms. Such phrases, however, tell us little of what the Chinese Nationalist Government is actually doing in Formosa to build up its strength, to correct its former shortcomings, and to improve the lot of the people of the island.

The purpose of the present volume is to present a dispassionate account of Chinese Nationalist rule in Formosa since 1945, with emphasis on recent internal developments and current problems. It is based in large part upon Chinese Nationalist sources, together with such other sources as are available, including first-hand reports. It does not aim to be exhaustive, but to give, in as balanced a manner as is possible in an area charged with controversy, a reasonably concise description of the Nationalist Government's record inside Formosa, with an appraisal of the strengths and weaknesses of its present position. It is issued under the auspices of the American Institute of Pacific Relations in the belief that it fairly presents some of the factors that must be taken into account in understanding the evolution of American policy toward Nationalist and Communist China.

The author of the present study, Dr. Fred W. Riggs, lived for many years in China. He was formerly a member of the research staff of the Foreign Policy Association, and is now with the Public Administration Clearing House in New York. In preparing this study he has had the benefit of advice and criticism from a number of persons with special knowledge of Formosa, whose aid has been of great value in revising the manuscript. Special thanks are due to Mr. Joseph W. Ballantine and Dr. Han Lih-wu for comments and information. The author, however, is solely responsible for all statements of fact or opinion in the volume.

WILLIAM L. HOLLAND

Executive Vice Chairman

American Institute of Pacific Relations

New York, May 27, 1952

Contents

[vii]

PART III: ECONOMIC

PART IV: SOCIAL

APPENDICES

FORMOSA
under Chinese
Nationalist Rule

CHAPTER ONE

Formosa: A Key Question

In current political controversies public attention in the United States has been focused upon a little known island in the western Pacific. During the four centuries since Portuguese navigators chanced upon the "Beautiful Island," Formosa has often figured as an object of international dispute. But it was not until it provided a retreat for the Chinese Nationalist Government of Chiang Kai-shek that Taiwan—to use its Chinese name—became the object of world-wide interest.

Rival Chinese Governments

Interest in Formosa arises from the consequences of events on the Chinese mainland. It is only as the headquarters of a contender for power on the mainland, and of a government recognized by the United States as the legal claimant to that power, that Taiwan has attracted global attention. The Korean crisis has heightened the role of Formosa as a major element in the world political struggle. But once the problems of Korea and China have been resolved, Formosa will subside once more into the relative obscurity from which it has so recently emerged.

Had the Nationalists retained control of the Chinese mainland, no controversy could have arisen concerning

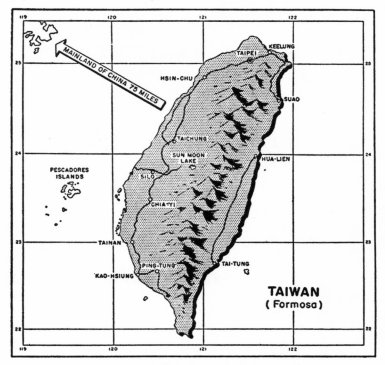

Source: Mutual Security Agency.

the implementation of the Cairo Declaration of 1943, which pledged the restoration of Formosa to "China." The dilemma posed by the rival claims of the governments of Chiang Kai-shek and Mao Tse-tung was further complicated by the aggression of North Korean forces in June 1950. When President Truman, on June 27, announced measures to deal with this situation, he simultaneously proclaimed the "neutralization" of Formosa and instructed the Seventh Fleet to implement this policy. At the same time he declared that the "determination of the future status of Formosa must await the restoration of security in the Pacific, a peace settlement with Japan, or consideration by the United Nations." Later, on July 19, Mr. Truman made clear that the United States had "no territorial ambitions whatever" regarding Formosa, and sought no special position or privileges there. The United States has continued, however, to extend diplomatic recognition to the Nationalist Government, and has consistently objected to linking the political demands of the Chinese Communists to the issue of aggression in Korea.

Nevertheless all proposals for resolving the Korean conflict have involved, in one way or another, the future of Formosa. The Chinese Communists have stated on numerous occasions that they would not consent to any political settlement for Korea which did not include the withdrawal of the Seventh Fleet from Formosan waters and, in effect, the termination of American assistance to the Nationalist Government. American support of the Nationalist Government has been the object of criticism in several countries with which the United States wishes to remain on friendly terms. History has forced the United States into a position in which there appears to be no possible policy toward Formosa that does not involve some unfavorable consequences.

US Policy: Opposing Trends

Two opposing trends have become manifest in American public opinion and in the Administration's record in dealing with this knotty question. The first favors a policy of non-intervention in the Chinese civil conflict, i.e., a hands-off attitude regarding Formosa. In support of this position it is argued that the Chinese Communists, however distasteful their internal practices and their international orientation may be, have in fact taken over control of the great bulk of China, and that no Far Eastern policy which fails to come to terms with this fact is realistic. The internal weaknesses of the Kuomintang regime have led some American observers to question the value of further reliance on the Chinese Nationalists as an instrument to contain or throw back the Communists on the mainland of Asia. These doubts were given their most explicit formulation in the United States White Paper on China,[1] issued in August 1949, and were apparently responsible for the Administration's decision, formulated in President Truman's statement on January 5, 1950, that "The United States will not pursue a course which will lead to involvement in the civil conflict in China. Similarly the United States Government will not provide military aid and advice to the Chinese forces on Formosa."[2]

The argument in favor of extending diplomatic recognition, on certain conditions, to Peking has lost ground as a result of the Chinese Communist intervention in Korea, while the recognition of Mao's regime by Britain, India and other states has increased the obstacles to unity among the non-Communist nations.

An opposite trend has reflected the view that the Kuomintang government, with all its weaknesses, constitutes the chief potential ally of the United States in dealing with a Communist regime on the mainland which, because of its role in the expansion of Soviet power and influence in Asia, should be vigorously opposed. This view has also been reinforced by the contention—first trenchantly presented to the public in General Douglas MacArthur's controversial message to the Veterans of Foreign Wars on August 27, 1950—that from the military standpoint the safeguarding of Taiwan as an element in a

---

1. *United States Relations with China,* Department of State Publication 3573, Far Eastern Series 30, 1949.
2. *Department of State Bulletin,* January 16, 1950, p. 79.

chain of island bases ringing the western Pacific is essential to the safety of the United States. Reported improvements in the military, political and economic situation within Formosa reinforced the position of those who advocated policies in line with these views. As a minimum they urged that Formosa should be safeguarded from Communist attack and that the continuance of the Nationalist Government should be ensured. As a maximum they recommended that the troops of Chiang Kai-shek be assisted to reconquer the mainland, or, at least, to harass the Communist armies in order to deflect Peking from hostile activities in Korea, Indochina and elsewhere.

The first important victory of this second school of thought was the President's directive of June 27, 1950. Though admittedly of an emergency nature, tied to the exigencies of the Korean conflict, this decision placed the direct weight of American military resources behind the Nationalists in Formosa. The President subsequently emphasized the temporary character of the decision when he stated on August 31 that the Seventh Fleet would be withdrawn upon settlement of the Korean conflict. Meanwhile, however, the dispatch of a military mission to Taipei in the summer of 1950, leading to a decision to furnish substantial military aid to Chiang Kai-shek, and the assignment early in 1951 of a military advisory group at the Generalissimo's headquarters, appeared to confirm a more long-range commitment to reinforce the Kuomintang position.

Some Americans hoped that a third way could be found to avoid the dangers implicit in either of the courses outlined above. They looked hopefully to Hongkong for evidence that Chinese liberals would form an effective Third Force which might be supported as a means of overthrowing the Communists without placing any reliance on the

Nationalists. Others hoped that similar results might be achieved in Formosa itself if Chiang Kai-shek could be induced to withdraw in favor of some new, popularly chosen leader. Finally, some observers, thinking primarily of the Formosan people themselves, advocated that the island be placed under some form of United Nations trusteeship, or that the local population be permitted, by plebiscite, to choose its own future destiny, thereby removing the island from its central position in the maelstrom of international rivalries. So far, however, none of these alternative courses appears to have gained much support among those responsible for the framing of American policy.

After the Chinese Communists intervened in Korea, and increasingly after the withdrawal of General MacArthur from his Far Eastern commands, the question of American policy toward Formosa came up for intensive public scrutiny. In his speech to Congress on April 19, 1951, General MacArthur called for a policy which would permit the Nationalists to make a military contribution to the struggle against the Chinese Communists. Secretary of Defense George C. Marshall subsequently told the Senate committees investigating MacArthur's dismissal that the primary aim of the forces on Taiwan should be to prevent the island from falling under Communist control, rather than to carry out aggressive actions on the Chinese mainland.[3]

When Secretary of State Dean Acheson appeared before the Senate group, he confirmed that United States policy called for safeguarding the island from Communist control. He added that the Administration had always considered that Formosa had strategic value and should not be allowed to fall into hostile hands, but that prior to June 27, 1950, it had not been prepared to use American armed

3. *New York Times,* May 14, 1951.

forces to prevent such a development.[4] Agreement appeared to have been reached, therefore, that United States policy would be directed toward the prevention of Communist control of Formosa. But the extent to which the Nationalists should be supported and utilized as part of the collective defense system against Soviet aggression, and as a possible means of overthrowing the Peking regime, had not been determined by the end of 1951.

On May 18, 1951, Dean Rusk, Assistant Secretary of State for Far Eastern Affairs, declared that the Nationalist Government on Formosa "more authentically represents the views of the great body of the people of China" than the Communist regime in Peking.[5] Some observers saw in this speech evidence that the Administration was moving toward fuller support for Chiang Kai-shek and stronger pressure against the "People's Government" of Mao Tse-tung. The State Department, however, promptly announced that the Rusk speech did not represent anything new in American Far Eastern policy. Nevertheless the Administration's proposals for foreign aid in its omnibus bill for the 1951–52 fiscal year included over $300 million for Taiwan, a third of the total allotted to the whole Far East.

Kuomintang Reforms

Clearly if basic decisions regarding American policy toward Formosa are to be made intelligently, it is essential that more information should be available, not only about the complex international political setting in which the decision is made, but also about the domestic situation in Taiwan itself. Such information may make it possible to determine to what extent the Kuomintang has remedied those inner weaknesses from which it suffered during its

4. *New York Times*, June 2, 1951, pp. 4 and 5; June 3, 1951, p. 64.
5. *New York Times*, May 19, 1951.

last years on the mainland. Even Chinese supporters of the Nationalist cause have conceded that, as Dr. Han Lih-wu put it, the "National Government of recent years left much to be desired," [6] but they assert that the government has now turned over a new leaf and that defects apparent on the mainland are rapidly being corrected on Formosa.

A study of recent developments will throw light on the potential military strength of the Nationalists, both for defense of the island and for possible action across the channel. It will also reveal the extent to which the political, economic and social policies now being followed in Taiwan may add to or subtract from the support that the Kuomintang might expect to win in the event of future mainland operations. The following study of internal developments in Formosa since the war is primarily intended to make generally available the kind of data which may shed light on the future prospects of the Nationalist regime.

At the same time this study may be useful in several other connections. The development of Taiwan under the Japanese, and the subsequent evolution of the island under Chinese Nationalist rule with substantial aid from the United States—notably through the Economic Cooperation Administration—may, as a case study, illuminate some of the problems encountered in American-sponsored programs for technical assistance to underdeveloped countries. In particular, experience in Formosa may offer some useful guides for future development programs elsewhere in Asia. Moreover, the records achieved on the island may be of considerable political importance in paving the way

6. Han Lih-wu, *Taiwan Today* (Taipei, Hwa Kuo Publishing Co., 1951), p. 18.

for other projects. Finally, this study may serve a purpose in presenting information about a relatively little known island and people whose history is not without its own intrinsic interest.

PART ONE

MILITARY

CHAPTER TWO

An Island Fortress?

The story of the defeat by the Communists of the four million troops in the Nationalist army on the mainland is well known. The rapid Communist conquest in April 1950 of Hainan island—a last bastion which the Kuomintang had promised to hold in a bitter and reinvigorated defense—disillusioned many who had hoped that adversity would transform the fighting caliber of the Nationalists. Nevertheless, Nationalist Premier Chen Cheng told the Legislative Yuan on October 2, 1950 that the government "voluntarily withdrew from Hainan; the forces being further concentrated for the defense of Taiwan." During the previous six months, he added, "six armies, 24 divisions, two fort commands, the Chusan Defense Headquarters and the Central China, Southwest and Southeast Commands, together with their subsidiary organs, a total of 89 units, were disbanded. . . . The remaining units have all undergone regrouping and their training has been further invigorated." As a result of better pay and other reforms, Chen said, "Marked improvements in the fighting strength, discipline and morale of the armed forces can be observed." [1]

In July 1950 General MacArthur himself went to For-

1. *Modern China* (Taipei), November 1950, p. 88.

mosa to observe the military position. He told the Senate Armed Services and Foreign Relations Committees on May 3, 1951, that he had found a half million troops composed of "excellent" personnel. They were "exactly the same," he said, as the "Red troops I am fighting. They have a good morale. Their material equipment is spotty. They lack artillery. They lack trucks. They lack a great many of the modern refinements. They are capable of being made into a very excellent force." [2]

US Military Aid

Pursuant to a recommendation made by General Mac-Arthur, a group of officers led by Brigadier General Alonzo P. Fox, Deputy Chief of Staff for the Far East Command, was subsequently sent to Formosa, where it compiled a comprehensive report on local military capacities and needs. In accordance with the recommendations of this report, Washington began to ship military supplies to Formosa in December 1950, after the Chinese Communists had intervened in force in Korea. On January 30, 1951, the United States formally notified Taipei that it would provide assistance under the Mutual Defense Assistance Program which might be used by Formosa to "maintain its internal security or its legitimate self-defense."

The terms of the proposed assistance arrangement were accepted by Taipei on February 9. Major General William C. Chase was chosen to head a military advisory group which arrived in Formosa on May 1. General Chase had acquired his reputation as a military leader when he commanded the First Cavalry Division during the liberation of Manila, but he had not previously had any experience in dealing with the Chinese. The scale of the military aid program may be judged from the fact that $90 million had

2. *New York Times*, May 4, 1951.

been spent by June 30, 1951, while over $200 million was scheduled for the year 1951–52.

From this it is clear that American officials considered the Chinese troops on Formosa an important potential anti-Communist force, even though American plans called solely for their utilization in the defense of the island. Since the report of the Fox mission has not been made public, it is possible to arrive at an estimate of the military potential of Formosa only by weighing Nationalist claims against the evidence of independent civilian observers.

Generalissimo Chiang Kai-shek on May 16, 1951 told reporters that a counteroffensive from Formosa against the mainland would force the Chinese Communists to curtail their aggressive activities in Korea. He went on, however, to state that "It would take six months for us to start the large-scale counteroffensive after necessary and adequate equipment and supplies are available in Formosa." [3]

Size of Nationalist Forces

Referring to the size of his army, Chiang has estimated that 500,000 men were in training. Others have given different reports, some going as high as 800,000. General MacArthur gave Congress the figure of 600,000. By comparing a number of accounts, it may be conservatively estimated that the Taiwan forces in mid-1951 included:

Army (ground forces)	345,000
Navy	45,000
Air Force	70,000
Combined Service Forces	20,000
Political officers and garrison	120,000
Total	600,000

A substantial part of the ground forces consisted of diseased, undernourished and overage soldiers. The high pro-

3. *New York Times*, May 17, 1951.

portion of older soldiers was said to be due to the fact that these men were assigned, on the mainland, to rear area, instead of front line, duty and consequently were more readily evacuated to Formosa. Whether this account is true or not, there seems to be agreement that not all the ground force troops could be made into combat effectives, although guesses as to the number of potential effectives vary between 200,000 and 300,000.[4]

A further serious limitation on the size of the Nationalist army stems from the fact that it is recruited almost exclusively from mainlanders, and is constantly being depleted by age, sickness and death. An estimated 25,000 were lost because of disease during 1950 and 1951. Lack of drugs and equipment, disregard for sanitation and inefficient administration by the Combined Service Forces are blamed for the high incidence of tuberculosis, malaria and dysentery, which lower the vitality of troops that do not succumb to killer diseases.

There has been considerable talk of filling the reduced ranks of the Nationalist armies by recruits drawn from Formosa's indigenous population of about six million. However, after the tragic events of 1947, in which hostility between Formosans and the mainland Chinese administration reached dangerous heights, the Kuomintang authorities were obviously reluctant to entrust local persons with arms. For their part, the Formosans were eager to receive military training on condition that they would have to fight only for their own interests, but they showed no enthusiasm about taking part in mainland operations.

At one time, when the safety of Formosa itself appeared most threatened, a program was inaugurated to train and

4. Cf. report by Michael James, *New York Times,* May 7, 1951; and Robert S. Elegant, "How Good is Chiang's Army?," *The Reporter,* December 25, 1951, pp. 17-20.

equip three divisions of native Formosans, and the train-ing of 4,500 non-commissioned officers was begun. Because of their high literacy level, these men learned more rapidly than mainland Chinese and were enthusiastic about their training. By August 1951 the program was abandoned—ostensibly for lack of funds—and Formosans were mustered out of service.

It is also alleged that the higher living standards of the Formosans not only made them more costly to maintain but promoted envy and dissatisfaction among mainland soldiers. Thus the Formosans had to receive more money in order to support their families, while the mainlanders obviously could not remit funds to relatives left behind. Again, the Formosans had acquired the habit of a daily hot bath, which entailed additional expense for fuel and required facilities not made available to the Chinese troops.

A new program of conscription of Formosan youths for basic training was subsequently inaugurated. Information about the size and potentiality of this force is not available at this writing, but it seems clear that it does not amount to more than a few thousand men. In any event, even if the Formosan manpower pool were heavily tapped during major operations, it is apparent that it could not long stand up against the vast resources in manpower of the mainland itself.

If Nationalist troops should effect a landing on the mainland, it is an open question how the manpower situ-ation would be affected. If, as the Kuomintang leaders maintain, great numbers of mainland dissidents should promptly rally to their banners, then their army might grow by leaps and bounds. On the other hand, should Communist authority and discipline over the local popu-lation prove firm, the Kuomintang might find its own forces dwindling as men deserted in order to try to return to their original homes.

Military Equipment

With regard to equipment, Philip Potter reported in January 1951 [5] that all services had great deficiencies but the Army was especially lacking in materiel because it was forced to abandon most of its resources on the mainland, including virtually all of its artillery. It managed to salvage 1,000 tanks but these were considered obsolete—consisting mainly of World War II M-5s and 4s equipped with 37-millimeter weapons or Shermans with 75s. Fuel, parts and ammunition shortages kept these immobilized, however, and many were dug in along the shore line as fixed defenses.

Some 60-millimeter mortars were produced in Formosa but heavier mortars, bazookas and ammunition were in gravely short supply. Men in training often carried wooden rifles and soldiers practicing on the firing range got only seventeen rounds apiece. Available rifles consisted of various American, Japanese and Chinese types. The soldiers were reported to be, on the whole, well fed as compared with their previous standards, obtaining a ration of about 2,500 calories a day. Their uniforms, generally speaking, were ragged, however, and many thousands had no shoes.

The Air Force in 1951 was said to number eight to ten groups, using perhaps 300 to 600 World War II planes—fighters, C-47 transports and light bombers. According to Hanson W. Baldwin, military analyst,[6] less than one-third of these were operational, and lack of spare parts, poor maintenance and limited gasoline supplies made it impossible that this force could provide effective air cover

5. *Baltimore Sun,* January 18, 1951.
6. *New York Times,* April 2, 1951.

for a mainland invasion. The Air Force flying school at Kangshang was said to train about 350 pilots every eighteen months, although students got only 160 hours of flying time as compared with 200 required of US pilots during World War II.

The Navy had in 1951 about seventy major vessels—LST and destroyer escort type—and numerous smaller craft. About a fourth of the naval personnel were officers. The Navy had been carrying out some drills in amphibious landing techniques. According to Hanson Baldwin [7] it could blockade part of China's coast, especially Shanghai, but could not stage a large-scale amphibious attack on the mainland.

The Human Organization

Limitations of a technical character are compounded by defects in the human organization of Formosa's armed forces. For example, an exceptionally high proportion of each service consists of officers. This has been justified on the ground that the officers will be needed after the "return to the mainland." At present, however, they add to the cost of maintaining the Army without contributing much to combat effectiveness. Meanwhile many officers, without men under their command, are free to engage in political intrigues.

The Air, Ground and Naval Forces maintain their highly autonomous character and are not trained for the kind of combined operation that would be necessary both for defense of the island and for invasion of the mainland. Inter-service rivalry is augmented by long-standing personal and clique antagonisms. One of these has recently come to the attention of the American public with the dismissal by the Chiang government of Lieutenant General P. T. Mow from his post as Air Force procurement officer

7. *Ibid.*

in Washington. Without discussing the intricacies of this case, it may be said that it reflects the culmination of a long and bitter struggle between Mow—one-time head of the Chinese Air Force—and its present head, Lieutenant General Chou Chih-jou, who was largely responsible for his predecessor's displacement.

Chiang Kai-shek, jealous of his personal eminence, continues to limit the authority of potentially strong leaders through the strategic appointment of his personal followers. The most notable example of this weakness appears to be in the restrictions imposed upon Lieutenant General Sun Li-jen—Virginia Military Institute-trained soldier who distinguished himself under General Joseph Stilwell in the Burma campaign during World War II— now nominally Commander-in-Chief of the ground forces. In practice, however, observers report that he has little real authority and is largely limited to supervising the training of the men.

American observers have been enthusiastic about the training being given at Fengshan under Sun's command. During an eighteen-hour day the men have individual instruction, two hours of physical training, drill in firing all infantry arms and practice of extended formation techniques, with special emphasis on camouflage, mortar firing and infiltration tactics. But this training program can be given to only a small part of the total armed forces. Other observers have been sharply critical of what they considered the unimaginative and mechanical way in which training has been conducted.

Real military control is said to be exercised by Chiang through his Army Chief of Staff, Lieutenant General Chou Chih-jou, who, as noted above, also commands the Air Force, and through his trusted premier, General Chen Cheng. General Chou was a close associate of Mme.

Chiang Kai-shek during World War II and directed the National Aeronautics Affairs Commission. Under his direct authority are four commanders responsible for the four military districts into which Formosa has been divided. General Sun has practically no authority over these men. The mechanized forces are under direct command of Chiang's second son, Chiang Wei-kuo.

A second major limitation on General Sun's authority results from the establishment of a "political commissar" system under Major General Chiang Ching-kuo, eldest son of the Generalissimo, who heads a Political Department in the Ministry of National Defense. He reports directly to his father and has under his command an extensive hierarchy of officers reaching down into the lowest echelons of the armed services with two assigned to each platoon. These men supervise recreational and indoctrinational activities and have promoted a campaign known as the "Overcoming Difficulties Movement" to induce soldiers to grow vegetables and livestock to supplement their rice rations. They have also done good work in combating illiteracy.

The most important function of this department, however, appears to be checking on the political reliability of officers and men. Directives initially issued by Soviet-trained Chiang Ching-kuo instructed his subordinates to establish a system of "thought control," but later the phrase was changed to the presumably more innocuous "reporting on activities." Even in military training, General Sun's chief remaining function, Chiang Ching-kuo appears to have intervened to a large extent. It is also said that these political officers exercise substantial influence in the promotion and demotion of line officers. American observers consider that this system undermines authority and efficiency within the armed forces and stimulates an atmosphere of fear and mutual distrust. The operations of Chiang Ching-kuo's men extend all the way to the top; General Sun Li-jen is said to be shadowed and some of his close friends have been accused of Communism, possibly in order to discredit Sun himself.

A third means of limiting General Sun's powers has been through the establishment of an independent combined supply board under Premier General Chen Cheng's Executive Yuan. This board, apparently none too efficient in its methods of caring for the limited material available, is in a position to impose embarrassing restrictions on the Army command. Despite these limitations the position of training leaders is of long-run strategic importance because a group of new officers owing personal loyalty to Sun will emerge in the course of time. Nevertheless, it seems apparent that the present human organization of the armed forces on Taiwan is not conducive to effective military action.

Potential Nationalist Strength

What can be done to transform the existing military establishment into an effective defense force, to say nothing of an instrument for attack? A group of American retired officers, headed by Rear Admiral Charles M. Cooke, Jr., is working under the aegis of a company known as Commerce International of China, which has been employed by Chiang since early in 1950 to assist in obtaining supplies for the Nationalists, as well as to provide advice and other services. One member of this group is reported to have said that a mainland invasion would be impossible without "100 per cent assistance logistically as well as air cover and naval transport." [8] In financial terms, Admiral Cooke is reported to have said that a $250 million military

8. Philip Potter in *Baltimore Sun*, January 19, 1951.

aid program coupled with American supervision would be enough to create an effective striking force.

Although the report of General Fox's mission has not been made public, accounts circulating in Taipei state that it indicated the Nationalists could be efficiently re-equipped for $400 million. If the army only were to be rearmed, with the United States supplying air and naval support in any future action, $100 million might be adequate, the Fox report was rumored to have said.[9]

In the light of these reports, it is evident that the military aid furnished by the United States in 1951 could do little more than assist the Formosan regime to gird for its own defense. On August 19, 1951 Secretary of State Dean Acheson reported that approximately $90 million in arms and ordnance had been given the Chiang regime, and that an additional $300 million was scheduled for the current fiscal year.[10] Later figures show $217 million as the amount of military aid for fiscal 1951–52.

Apart from financial aid to help equip the Nationalist forces, extensive reorganization of the structure of command would be necessary for an effective fighting force to emerge. Generalissimo Chiang on May 2, 1951, following the establishment of the US Military Assistance Advisory Group (MAAG) in Formosa, informed General Chase that all echelons of the armed services would be open to any task the group set. There would be no interference, he said, with the work of the new US advisers. Past experi-

9. Michael James in *New York Times,* April 22, 1951. On May 5 James reported that the Fox mission "is reliably understood" to have suggested an appropriation of $500 million if the Formosan forces were to reach their "full potential efficiency."

10. *Department of State Bulletin,* September 3, 1951, p. 398. According to the *New York Times,* January 2, 1952, Formosa received $81.2 million in 1950–51 and over $200 million for 1951–52.

ence, however, has made American military observers doubt whether such promises, made on ceremonial occasions, would mean much when Western advisers tangled with the intricacies of Kuomintang personal politics. General Chase himself has assumed a cautious attitude, telling reporters that the reorganization of the Chinese military establishment was "none of our business." He stated that it had not yet been determined how far down in the chain of command his advisory group would operate. In practice it is clear that the powers of the MAAG are essentially advisory. It lacks authority to bring about fundamental reorganization, such as the elimination of excess officers, or the curtailment of the powers of the ubiquitous political officers. Efforts to restrict the role of Chiang Ching-kuo's political men have, indeed, been strongly resisted, although an agreement was reached to appoint an "adviser" in the Political Department of the Defense Ministry. Other inherent difficulties, such as the lack of adequate food for the troops, cannot be overcome directly by the advisory group, although it is taking some steps to assist the Formosan program for increasing productivity, especially in such fields as deep sea fishing.

There appears to be some confusion as to the exact size of the military aid group. On June 24, 1951 General Chase gave the mission's size as 1,250 persons. The Department of State announced on August 20, 1951 that a 600-man military mission was on the island. Reports from the field in October, however, intimated that only 200 men were actually on duty. An Associated Press dispatch from Taipei on March 18, 1952 asserted that 360 officers and men were in the MAAG, but that plans called for doubling the size of the group during 1952. On April 9, 1952 Secretary of the Navy Dan A. Kimball urged a five-fold increase of the 400-man MAAG.

It becomes apparent, therefore, that whatever the potential effectiveness of the Chinese armed forces on Formosa might be, as of early 1952 they could contribute little toward any operations on the mainland beyond limited activities, such as partial blockades, raids and perhaps assistance to, and coordination of, mainland guerrillas. This fact has been acknowledged by Chiang himself. In a statement in March 1952 he called for aid to carry out such guerrilla and commando raids on the mainland, as a prelude to a resumption of power which would not take place for some years thereafter.

The chief task to which the Nationalist forces could apply themselves, however, would be the defense of Formosa itself. The water barrier provides a formidable obstacle to any land power, such as the Chinese Communist regime, enabling a relatively weak organization to maintain a defense of the island. But the same water obstacle also impedes any insular power from recovering the mainland. In this respect Formosa differs geostrategically from the far hinterland which served Free China as a base during the war with Japan. It follows that there are fairly good prospects that the Chiang government can defend its island bastion, although even in this task it is also clear that it must rely on substantial external aid, both in building up its army and economy, and in providing an air and sea shield against attack. It is also apparent that the Kuomintang can have little prospect of a successful action on the mainland unless the Communist regime were itself tottering on the verge of collapse from its own internal weaknesses.

A particular dilemma for American policy arises from the fact that the morale of Chiang's men is to a large extent sustained by the conviction that they are preparing for an imminent return to the mainland and their homes

and families, about whom they are naturally deeply concerned. Were they to be told that their main function was
to defend the island in which they live as strangers, the
effect on morale might be such as to make even this relatively limited task impossible. The question may well be
asked how long the Nationalist soldiers can be kept keyed
up to a high pitch of preparedness for an eventuality that
may appear to recede ever farther into the future.

PART TWO

POLITICAL

CHAPTER THREE

The Apparatus of Control

If Chiang Kai-shek and his Formosan government are ever to recover the mainland, it is apparent that they will need not only an effective military force, but also a political organization capable of backing up the army and winning support from the mainland population. The reliability of the Nationalist political structure for these ends may be gauged by its internal organization and by its relationship to the indigenous people of Formosa.

In discussing the Nationalist political regime, one is tempted to form judgments in terms of American values, such as "democracy," "civil liberties" and "individualism." Whatever the usefulness in the abstract of such criteria, the emphasis here must be on the values held by the Chinese themselves. It is apparent that in certain of their policies, such as the introduction of village and *hsien* elections, the Taipei authorities have sought to win approval in the United States. The significant test of such innovations, however, is their effect on the attitudes of the Formosans. Do they provide a means to help achieve the "felt needs" of the population, or do they constitute measures of a formalistic type introduced from above without relevance or responsiveness to local interests?

In judging Chiang Kai-shek's government, therefore, we

may begin by examining its constitutional position, its integrity and efficiency as an administration, its ability to win loyalty and active support from various elements of the population, especially the Formosans themselves, and its record in meeting the various technical problems of mobilizing the economy, operating social services and maintaining law and order.

Constitutional Position

The inner structure of the Nationalist Government is determined by the preeminent position of its leader, Generalissimo Chiang Kai-shek. In accordance with the constitution adopted by the Kuomintang-controlled Constituent National Assembly on Christmas Day, 1946, and the electoral law of March 31, 1947, Chiang Kai-shek was elected President of the Chinese Republic on April 19, 1948 by the first National Assembly. Contrary to the wishes of the dominant organization inside the Kuomintang, however, General Li Tsung-jen, well known as a leader of the Kwangsi faction, was subsequently elected to the vice presidency.

On January 21, 1949, as Nationalist military resistance in North China crumbled before the advancing Communists, Chiang Kai-shek "withdrew" from the presidency, leaving Vice President Li to serve as Acting President. From retirement in Chekiang, his home province, Chiang directed the concentration of troops personally loyal to him, and began to move them to Formosa together with quantities of military equipment. In April Nanking fell and the Generalissimo himself fled to Formosa together with important civil and military leaders, his personal followers and the government's reserves of gold, silver and foreign currency. Meanwhile Acting President Li's government moved south and west, where it met final defeat by the end of the year. In Formosa, Chiang, although not titular head of the government, retained the position of leader of the Kuomintang and director-general of its Central Executive Committee, as well as the post of Chairman of the Emergency War Council.

From this somewhat anomalous position, Chiang began unofficially to resume the mantle of national leadership. On July 5, 1949 he told newspaper correspondents of his obligation and determination to lead the Chinese people in a great crusade against Communism. Five days later he met President Elpidio Quirino in the Philippines to discuss the possibility of a "Pacific Pact."

The legal position in Formosa was murky. A provincial government, composed chiefly of mainland Chinese, operated from Taipei under the direction of General Chen Cheng. Numerous Nationalist bureaus and government agencies, staffed with refugees, moved in from abandoned offices in Nanking and searched feverishly for quarters. Chiang Kai-shek resided in a mountain resort some fifteen miles from Taipei, where as party leader he directed Kuomintang activities. Clearance of policy with the mainland rump government of Li Tsung-jen became increasingly tenuous.

The Chinese Air Force under General Chou Chih-jou and the Navy under Admiral Kwei Yung-ching, operating directly under Chiang's control, in the autumn of 1949 imposed a partial "port closure" of the China coast and carried out hit-and-run air attacks on coastal cities. The United States, however, refused to recognize this action as a "blockade" since such recognition would have implied cognizance of the Peking government as a belligerent.

In December 1949 the fortunes of the Kuomintang regime reached their lowest ebb. On the seventh Li's migratory government abandoned Chengtu, its last sanctuary in West China. The next day Taipei was proclaimed the new Chinese temporary capital. But Acting President Li was absent, for he had flown to the United States to undergo an emergency operation. The beclouded political waters in Formosa began to precipitate. Pro-Li elements sought passage to Hongkong, while Chiang supporters on the mainland fled to Formosa. On December 17 Governor Chen Cheng was elevated to the premiership of the National Government as President of the Executive Yuan.

US Attitude

The mainland had fallen to the Communists. Chiang was preparing to reclaim the presidency and to make his "last ditch stand" on Formosa. But Washington anticipated a final catastrophe. On December 23 it issued its now famous Special Guidance policy directive No. 28 to information officers,[1] instructing them that if Formosa should be lost, its political and strategic significance was to be minimized. They were told to counter the "false impression" that the retention of Formosa would "save the Chinese Government," or "seriously damage the interests of either the United States or of other countries opposing communism."

The White Paper of August 1949 had paved the way for the expected denouement. On January 5, 1950 President Truman announced that the United States would not become involved in the Chinese "civil conflict." Washington had no wish to play the role of *deus ex machina* in this tragic drama. On the same day London recognized Peking as the seat of the government of China. New Delhi had already extended recognition the week before. The cause of the Nationalists appeared desperate indeed.

In this moment of high international tension the leaders of American foreign policy lost the initiative. Stalled at

1. Text in *New York Times,* June 2, 1951.

dead center, they waited while a new constellation of political forces took shape. Then, in June, the North Korean
invasion of South Korea whipped the American leviathan
once more into vigorous action. By this time pro-National-
ist and anti-Communist sentiment in the United States
had been heated explosively by a combination of domestic
partisan pressures and by Chinese Communist attacks on
American consular personnel and property.

The Korean spark touched off the explosion. On June
27 President Truman ordered the navy to "neutralize"
Formosa. Four days later General Douglas MacArthur was
conferring with Chiang on Taiwan. A month later the
State Department had changed its consulate-general in
Taipei to an embassy.

Chiang Kai-shek and Li Tsung-jen

But Chiang's battle for survival entailed not only his
struggle for American aid and recognition. It also involved
his perpetual campaign for supremacy over the cliques
that challenged his hegemony at home. Perhaps the most
important of his rivals was General Li Tsung-jen, the Acting President, who, as we have seen, sped to the United
States in December 1949. There Li made an open bid for
American support as the leader of a potential Third Force
between the Communists and the partisans of Chiang. He
arranged to have dinner with President Truman on March
2, 1950. But on March 1 the Generalissimo, responding to
"the people's will," proclaimed that he was resuming office
as President of China. A few days earlier General Li had
written to Chiang, "Without an election by the National
Assembly you have no legal ground to become again the
President of China." [2]

Despite the subsequent recognition of Chiang's admin-

2. *The Chinese World* (San Francisco), March 7, 1950.

istration by the State Department, Li has continued to insist that Chiang violated the Chinese Constitution by resuming the presidency. As recently as December 1, 1951, he addressed a memorandum to the State Department reaffirming his position. He subsequently announced that he had "a plan to return which I shall reveal in the near future." [3] But Chiang has attempted to minimize all prospects for an early return to power by his rival. Immediately upon his resumption of the presidency, Chiang instituted a comprehensive purge in which at least ninety high-ranking civil and military officials were arrested, some being executed, including the Vice Minister of National Defense.

Kuomintang Cliques

Chiang Kai-shek has always made the first criterion for his support of a subordinate the quality of personal loyalty, rather than ability or devotion to any particular political program. Individuals and groups with divergent ideas about national policy and from differing kinds of background gravitated naturally into rival cliques. Rather than give supreme leadership to any one of these factions, Chiang preferred to use them to check each other. No man could become powerful enough to win national recognition and preeminence because the leaders of another group would be aided by Chiang and placed in important positions where they could check the potential rival. Consequently no leader and no group could rule alone. In every showdown a claimant for power would finally have to turn to Chiang for help in order to retrieve a rapidly deteriorating situation.

The clique system within the Kuomintang has been the essential means by which Chiang Kai-shek maintained his

3. *New York Times,* December 6, 1951.

personal supremacy. But at the same time this system has made Chiang indispensable for the continuance of the party. The party has become his personal instrument, and his personal weaknesses and limitations have thereby been transmitted to the party and to the government and army.[4]

If no clique could rule without Chiang, the converse has also been true: Chiang could not rule without the co-operation of the cliques. This has been a serious weakness, since even when Chiang had strong and constructive ideas for national policy, the opposition of a clique could keep the program from leaving the drafting room.

Because only the political leaders most loyal to Chiang accompanied him to Formosa, while disaffected politicians either joined the Communists or went into exile abroad, it may be presumed that the Generalissimo's personal control of the Kuomintang and the government has been strengthened. Correspondingly, as his personal authority has been enhanced, Chiang has also been given an opportunity to exercise his powers of creative leadership in the reform and strengthening of the party and administration. The future of his regime may depend in large part on his ability to rise to this opportunity.

Party Reform

Responding to demands for reform, as well as to his enhanced personal authority, Chiang sanctioned the estab-

4. Chien Tuan-sheng, a leading Chinese authority, writes: "The leader of the Kuomintang is not only the head of its organization, but actually holds it together. Or to state it in another way, the Leader has allowed the party to be segmented so that he alone supplies the link between its several segments. It is in this all-important feature, rather than in its doctrine, or in its organization, or even in the social basis of its membership, that one can discover a key to the understanding of the Kuomintang." *The Government and Politics of China* (Cambridge, Harvard University Press, 1950), p. 132.

lishment of a Central Reform Committee in July 1950 to overhaul the basic structure of the party. A member of this group, Tsui Shu-chin, former professor of international law at the University of Peking and a member of the Legislative Yuan, has attributed the need for reform to three major factors: the prevalence of "unauthorized factions" which must be dissolved; the loss of control by the party over its members in the Legislative and Control Yuans; and the lack of discipline and loss of revolutionary spirit among party members.[5] But the loss of control in the legislative bodies results from animosities between rival factions. The same cause underlies loss of "revolutionary spirit," since the basic motivation of each faction has been its own quest for power. Idealistic and public-spirited Chinese who joined the party tended to become disillusioned and cynically aligned themselves with a clique, or else they resigned their memberships.

As a first step toward party reform the new committee, according to Professor Tsui, would permit "good" old members to retain their membership, but those guilty of the following acts must be purged: "treason, disloyalty to the party, violation·of party discipline, corruption, living a rotten life, desertion from official duty, wavering in devotion to party principles, and engagement in profiteering business." New members must be "absolutely loyal to the state and to the party." The role of the party in the government, Tsui pointed out, was no longer that of tutelage but was that of an "ordinary political party." In other words, the party could no longer "interfere directly with the official duties" of party members in legislative assemblies and administrative offices. Instead, these party members "are merely required to see that the people's assem-

5. *Modern China* (Taipei), October 1950, p. 27.

blies legislate according to the policies of the party or that the government adopt them as their official policies."

Among the specific aims of the reform plan promulgated by the new Committee in September 1950 were: (1) encouragement of private enterprise, opposition to monopolistic combinations, and transfer of government-operated light industries to private ownership; (2) workers' participation in the ownership and management of private enterprises; (3) more foreign investment and technical cooperation; (4) aid to tenant farmers through land reform, water conservancy and land reclamation; (5) development of local self-government and the promotion of civil rights; and (6) after return to the mainland, punishment for Communist leaders, amnesty for those who followed the Communists under duress, and permission to farmers to continue to work the land they had been tilling.[6]

Apart from certain ambiguities in these announced objectives, the general aims appear praiseworthy. Whether they can be implemented must depend upon whether the Kuomintang can establish real party discipline and reduce the particularisms and hostilities of the rival cliques.

It remains to be seen how the reform group will in practice go about eliminating the "unauthorized cliques." The central Executive and Supervisory Committees of the party have been suspended until after the reform has been completed. In the interim the Reform Committee is to frame plans while a new Committee of Supervision is to enforce the reforms. The latter group is composed of twenty-five veteran leaders of the party; the former of sixteen "younger men," chaired by Chiang Kai-shek. Gung-hsing Wang as-

6. *The Present Political Platform of the Kuomintang* (Taipei, September 1950), cited in Gung-hsing Wang, "Nationalist Government Policies, 1949–51," *Annals* of the American Academy of Political and Social Science, September 1951, pp. 214-15.

serts that the Reform Committee will "administer the Reform Plan." The group of elder statesmen, which he calls the "Committee of Supervision," is, in his words, to "supervise the administration." [7] Even if the younger men did produce an ideal reform plan, it is likely that the "veteran leaders" would cling to long-established behavior patterns and loyalties.

Shifts in the Political Pattern

Some important changes in the pattern of cliques may nevertheless result from external forces. Throughout the Kuomintang era there have been continuous and complex changes of this sort. One of the most influential factions, known as the Political Science Group, including many men of affairs with ability in finance and government, has been weakened by the move to Formosa. In June 1950 T. V. and T. L. Soong, H. H. Kung and Sun Fo were ousted from the Central Executive Committee of the Kuomintang and the Board of the Bank of China. Moreover, they were not living in Formosa.

But the men who controlled the Organization Department of the party and its secret police, known as the Bureau of Investigation and Statistics, appear to be strongly entrenched in Formosa. Called the CC Clique from the initials of the two brothers who guided it, Chen Li-fu and Chen Kuo-fu, this faction continues to exercise important influence in Kuomintang affairs, although there is some opinion that its strength has declined recently.

The way in which the jurisdiction of General Sun Li-jen, a man who has eschewed clique politics, has been circumscribed illustrates the continued power in Formosa of the chief military faction, known as the Whampoa Clique because its leading members were students under Chiang at

7. *Ibid.*, p. 213.

the famous Whampoa revolutionary academy. Among the members of the Reform Committee is Chiang Ching-kuo, the Generalissimo's son. He directs the political commissar and "thought control" system in the army, is Director of Party Affairs, and a leader of the Youth Corps. The power of the younger Chiang, according to various reports, appears to be steadily growing on the island and doubtless represents the emergence of a new faction which, as in earlier cases, reports directly to the Generalissimo. Indeed, it is the view of some observers that the Generalissimo has been placing increasing reliance on his sons in place of the older cliques.

The structure of power in Taiwan appears to have been subjected to considerable pressure during the fall of 1951. In July the Nationalist Government was not invited to San Francisco to participate in the signing of a peace treaty with Japan. It was peculiarly ironical that no representative of the people who had suffered most from Japanese aggression should have taken part in this historic event. The repercussions in Taipei were severe, including proffers of resignation during July by both the Prime Minister and the Foreign Minister. Criticisms of the Generalissimo increased, and other factors combined to jeopardize Chiang's leadership. He moved swiftly to safeguard his position. Some of his close associates were arrested. Several highly placed persons were executed during October and November, and the crushing of a "large red espionage underground" was announced.

Nevertheless the governmental picture on Formosa remains obscure. It is premature to seek a long-run pattern. Only time will show whether the foundations are being laid for a revitalized party and government. At the present moment, however, the system of cliques held in their undulating orbits by personal loyalty to Chiang does not appear to have been fundamentally changed, although the personal ties to Chiang may well have been strengthened by the move to Taiwan.

Some observers think that the only reform that could win widespread allegiance from the Chinese people would be some fundamental change which would shift the center of political gravitation away from Chiang, whose name is now associated with the defeated regime. For example, a widely representative assembly might choose new leadership which could reorganize the government on the basis of efficiency and responsibility to the public rather than of factional checks and balances. But in Formosa this could be accomplished only through the voluntary and sincere cooperation of Chiang himself. The task of persuading him to renounce personal power, which he equates with the welfare and destiny of China, and at the same time to give real support to the regime set up to succeed his own is one that has yet to be accomplished.

Yet there are certain new factors which do not completely rule out this possibility. The shock of defeat may have induced a mood of contrition and rededication among the Nationalist leaders which could lead to political miracles. The increasing military and economic support which the United States is giving to Formosa could be coupled with political pressures of a new kind. A major new influence is the island of Formosa itself, which confronts the Kuomintang politicians with an unprecedented kind of political, economic and psychological problem. The progressive administration of Governor K. C. Wu and the bracing impact of Formosans on the mainland Nationalist leadership may produce unexpected results.

CHAPTER FOUR

Nationalist Rule in Formosa

The stability of any government is tested by its ability to rule in the interests of its constituents. Popular support for the Kuomintang regime has been undermined by the willingness of many party leaders to put their own interests above those of the nation. Nowhere has this been more clearly revealed than in Formosa, yet the response of the people of Taiwan and the peculiar pressures of the world situation have compelled modifications in the behavior of the Nationalists which might conceivably lead to greater democracy and efficiency.

Formosa's Post-war Governors

In the half dozen years since VJ-Day, the island of Formosa has been administered by four governors, each of whom was appointed by Chiang Kai-shek, not primarily because of his ability to serve the people of the newly recovered province but chiefly because of his presumed capacity to fulfill some requirement of the Generalissimo. The first of these men was Chen Yi, a war lord to whom Chiang owed a debt of gratitude for a timely defection during the Northern Expedition in 1927. In the mood of victory over Japan, Formosa was considered both a fat piece of "war booty" and a "remote province." It was treated as such, the main aims of the administration appearing to be the payment of old political debts and the reaping of rewards.

By 1947, however, the scandals of Chen Yi's administration and particularly the massacre of March 1947 had attained world-wide notoriety. Struggling bitterly for supremacy on the mainland, Chiang desperately needed American support. Hoping to appease Washington and make a better impression on visiting Congressmen, Chiang relieved Chen and appointed in his stead the suave former ambassador to the United States, Wei Tao-ming. Chen was given a face-saving job and ultimately the governorship of Chekiang province. In January 1949, however, this opportunistic war lord secretly connived with Communist agents to surrender his province. Learning of the plot, Nationalist police arrested Chen and on June 18, 1950 a firing squad in Formosa brought to an end his career of duplicity and personal profiteering. Governor Wei, for his part, found his none too energetic efforts to improve the island's administration frustrated by some of Chen's henchmen who remained entrenched in important positions.

As 1948 drew to a close Chiang, facing defeat on the mainland, began to think about the possibilities of using Taiwan as a base for his last retreat. He needed a strong and reliable man to lay the foundations for his "impregnable bastion." Such a man was General Chen Cheng, competent and thoroughly loyal. The new governor assumed office on January 5, 1949 and at once began to substitute newly arrived refugee officials for the Chen Yi and Wei Tao-ming entourage, to carry out currency and rent reforms, and to prepare the basis for a new economic and political order.

Meanwhile Chiang Kai-shek himself came to the island and by the end of 1949 he was ready to proclaim the National Government in Taipei. He needed Chen for the more responsible post of President of the Executive Yuan. By this time it had also become clear to Chiang that he could not hope to defend the island from a threatened Communist attack, to say nothing of staging an ultimate comeback on the mainland, without the support of the Formosan population, among whom previous policy had produced widespread disaffection. K. C. Wu, Princeton-educated and one-time Mayor of Shanghai, was designated for the post of governor. Under his administration, and with American aid through ECA (later superseded by MSA, the Mutual Security Agency), there is little doubt that many improvements in the lot of the Formosans have begun to take place, among them increasing participation by local people in their own government. Out of necessity, and as a result of the superior technical and economic standards of the island built up by the Japanese, the Nationalists have learned to improve their administrative methods and have been compelled to pay more than lip service to the principle of democratic responsibility. This evolutionary process may be observed at closer range in the policies followed by the Nationalists and the reactions of the Formosans as they have worked themselves out since VJ-Day.

The Chen Yi Regime

The six million Chinese-descended natives of Formosa were generally enthusiastic at the prospect of returning to Chinese rule after half a century of colonial subjection to Japan. Their hopes were quickly crushed when the carpet-bagging administration of Chen Yi proceeded to take over systematically all industries and properties built by Japanese enterprise but, instead of developing them and restoring war-time damage, proceeded to enrich themselves through systematic plunder, selling basic raw materials and manufactured goods in the starved markets of the mainland and allowing productive resources to deteriorate. Rice and coal, bought at low fixed prices, were sold in China at fantastic profits. Native Formosans who had held secondary posts under the Japanese hoped to step into newly vacated managerial and executive positions, but found themselves pushed aside by mainlanders, or by one-time Formosans who had emigrated to the mainland —referred to derisively by the Formosans as "half-mountain men"—many of whom had ingratiated themselves with Chen Yi's clique during their stay in China.

Tension between Taiwanese and mainlanders mounted until, on February 28, 1947, an incident took place involving an attack by mainland police upon a native woman peddling cigarettes without the license demanded by the government's Monopoly Bureau. Thereupon an angry crowd formed and the officer fired, killing one of the bystanders. The police fled and the crowd burned vehicles belonging to the Monopoly Bureau. This incident precipitated a series of events characterized by mob violence and gunplay which culminated in the presentation of demands by responsible Formosan spokesmen and their nominal acceptance by the beleaguered Chen Yi. By March 6 most of the island was in the hands of Formosan leaders headed by a Settlement Committee. Meanwhile, however, Chen Yi had sought reinforcements from the mainland. On March 8 the reinforcements arrived and Chen Yi struck. Armed trucks patrolled the streets and Formosan leaders were systematically sought out and executed. For a long time thereafter Formosan oppositionists were seized, detained and often executed on charges of having participated in the uprising.[1]

1. For details see Memorandum on the Situation in Taiwan, *United States Relations with China* (Department of State Publication 3573, Far Eastern Series 30, 1949), pp. 923-38. See also George

Repercussions were not long in making themselves felt on the mainland, where anti-Chen Yi cliques and Formosan sympathizers were able on March 22 to obtain support from fifty-one members of the Kuomintang Central Executive Committee for a petition demanding the dismissal and punishment of Chen Yi. After a stormy debate, the committee adopted the petition. Chen Yi on March 24 submitted his resignation and Defense Minister General Pai Chung-hsi was sent to investigate the situation.

Apologists for Chen Yi pointed to certain extenuating circumstances: the extreme difficulty of administering an island disrupted by war and bombing, and by the withdrawal of key Japanese personnel; the lack of experience and training of the would-be Formosan leaders; the hostility, boycotts and sabotage employed by the embittered Taiwanese in their struggle against the new regime; and the natural anti-Formosan sentiment developed among the Chinese mainlanders because of past collaboration of Formosans with the Japanese.

Nevertheless the excesses of the Chen Yi regime were too flagrant to be explained away or excused. On April 22, 1947 Nanking, having the American reaction in mind, announced the appointment of Dr. Wei Tao-ming as the new governor. Although flagrant abuses were not so conspicuous during Wei's term of office as they had been under his predecessor, conditions remained bad. The disposal of removable wealth had been largely accomplished, so that the chief remaining means of personal enrichment consisted of various devices to squeeze current income out of the population. Many Formosan leaders had been "liquidated" or driven into exile, while those that remained

---

Kerr, "Formosa's Return to China," *Far Eastern Survey,* October 15, 1947, and "Formosa: The March Massacres," *Far Eastern Survey,* November 5, 1947.

had been terrorized into silent acquiescence. Wei Tao-ming, with his Western training and experience, paid particular attention to those matters which would impress the Americans who began more frequently to include Formosa in their Far Eastern itineraries.

The administration of Chen Cheng, whose selection was announced on December 30, 1948, was plagued by difficulties of a new kind, created by the influx of a flood of refugees: generals with their defeated or retreating troops; wealthy landlords and businessmen who feared the approaching Communists; and a swarm of government officials, secret police and camp followers. With them came their household valuables and between $200 and $300 million in gold reserves of the Nanking government. House rents and "key money" soared while rising prices intensified the difficulties of the local population.

Formosan Participation in Government

Against this general background the Kuomintang administration decided, as a result of local pressure and in the hope of winning American support, to grant concessions to the Formosans. Under Chen Yi, none of the commissioners—who head the departments of the provincial administration—had been Formosans. After Wei Tao-ming assumed office seven of the fifteen commissioners were Formosans. Local leaders, however, were not greatly impressed by this concession. Three of the seven were "half-mountain men," having spent the war years in Chungking, where they had attached themselves to Chen Yi. One of them, Chiu Nien-tai, held the post of Commissioner of Civil Affairs, equivalent to a European Ministry of the Interior, and served as provincial chairman of the Kuomintang. Another three were disliked by Taiwan nationalists because of their former close collaboration with the

Japanese. The seventh was of aboriginal extraction. Moreover, the key positions in control of finance, defense and propaganda were held by Chen Yi stalwarts. Notable among them was Yen Chia-ken, Finance Commissioner; Peng Meng-chih, Garrison Commander; Wang Min-ning, Police Commissioner; and Li Wan-chu, publisher of the official newspaper, the *Shin Sheng Pao*.

After K. C. Wu became governor the provincial commission was enlarged to include seventeen Formosans out of a total of twenty-three. Local critics, however, contended that the Taiwanese selected for these jobs were "mediocre" men and former collaborators. As before, the most important posts were retained by mainlanders and the Formosans were given responsibility for carrying out unpopular duties. Nevertheless, the mere fact that Taiwanese were included in such numbers among the chief provincial administrators was a significant development.

Comparable advances were made in the employment of civil service personnel. By June 1950, according to official data, there were 55 Formosans among 316 employees in senior posts, 780 out of 3,118 in second class positions and 15,476 out of 24,635 in third class jobs. Of 22,130 teaching personnel, 15,929 were Taiwanese. Of the total of 81,006 persons employed by the provincial government, Formosans accounted for 53,024.[2]

Of perhaps greater significance as a spearhead for Formosan development was the creation of a provincial People's Political Council (PPC) in which local leadership had an opportunity to emerge. The foundations for this step had been laid during the Japanese period in district assemblies, half of whose members were elected by local councils for cities, towns and villages, and the other half

2. Han Lih-wu, *Taiwan Today* (Taipei, Hwa Kuo Publishing Co., 1951), p. 30.

appointed by district governors. Although largely advisory in character, these bodies gave many Formosans some experience which provided a basis for their postwar activities.

Shortly after Chen Yi took over control of Formosa, he announced plans for the election of "Organs for Hearing the People's Opinion." Nine elected district and municipal councils would in turn designate a provisional provincial assembly. Only native Formosans would be eligible to vote and to run as candidates but two safeguards were provided to prevent embarrassment to the Kuomintang administration: the councils' powers were circumscribed and candidates had to fulfill conditions laid down by the government. In the event of a dispute between the Assembly and the governor, the latter made the final decision.

The first PPC met in May 1946 and immediately became a sounding board for violent denunciations of the provincial administration. A number of voices soon became conspicuous among those attacking the government. Preeminent was the lawyer Wang Tien-teng, who was subsequently arrested, charged with inciting rebellion. He was tried and sentenced, then released, but subsequently killed while "resisting arrest" in March 1947, during Chen Yi's suppression of the Formosan autonomy movement. Nevertheless, in successive semi-annual sessions the PPC became a stronghold of Formosan local sentiment.

Although relations between the Formosans and mainland Chinese continued to be tense, after 1947 surface manifestations of underlying hostility declined—partly because of growing caution on the part of the Formosans after some of their leading spokesmen had been imprisoned or executed and partly because of the government's increasingly conciliatory policy. Nevertheless, periodic arrests continued on a small scale. In the fall of 1949, after

Chiang Kai-shek had moved his personal headquarters to the island and mainland refugees had flooded in, stern measures were taken against opposition elements. According to Joshua Liao, a Formosan leader, more than 10,000 persons were arrested.

Local Self-Government

As a counterbalance to the mass purges, Governor Chen Cheng's administration had begun to prepare for the election of councils and magistrates which would be endowed with more precise constitutional status and greater powers than the provisional assemblies elected in 1946. A Committee for the Planning and Study of Local Government in Taiwan was established which drew up a set of regulations. After adoption by the Provincial Government and revision in the PPC, they were approved by the National Government and promulgated on April 5, 1950.

Before new elections could be held, however, it was decided to modify the administrative district system. Taiwan had been divided into eight counties (*hsien*) and nine municipalities. Great discrepancies existed between the size of the populations of these units. On the demand of the Provincial Assembly, the government proceeded with studies already under way and in August 1950 a redemarcation scheme was promulgated, involving the establishment of sixteen counties and five municipalities. Several of the larger former counties together with small cities were subdivided into smaller *hsien* units.[3]

3. The *hsien*, as redemarcated, consist of Taipei, Taoyuan, Hsinchu, Miaoli, Taichung, Changhua, Tunlin, Chia-i, Tainan, Kaohsiung, Pintung, Taitung, Hualien, Yilan, Nantou and Penghu. The cities of Taipei, Taichung, Tainan, Kaohsiung and Keelung were retained as independent municipalities. Eugene H. C. Wang, "Readjustment of the Administrative Districts in Taiwan," *Modern China* (Taipei), October 1950, pp. 36-38; and Han Lih-wu, *op. cit.*, pp. 35-38.

On the basis of the new regulations and revised districts, elections were then held under the general supervision of a joint committee established by the provincial government and the PPC. Elections for city and *hsien* councils were conducted in three groups as local preparations were completed, the first being in July 1950 and the last in January 1951. The balloting for mayors and magistrates began in October 1950 and the last group was completed by the end of April 1951. Simultaneously elections were also held for heads and representative bodies in towns and villages within the larger administrative districts.

Among the election regulations promulgated by the government were the following: people holding office were forbidden to "manipulate" the elections; a quota of seats on councils was to be reserved for women and tribesmen in the mountains; election expenses of candidates were to be limited; bribery or special inducements to voters were prohibited; and candidates were not to coerce voters or slander their opponents.[4] After the elections had been held Yang Chao-chia, Civil Affairs Commissioner, announced that the new councils would lay a solid foundation for the orderly advancement of self-rule. He declared that the elections were noteworthy for the "complete absence of Government influence in the choice of candidates, the enthusiasm with which the constituents exercised their voting rights and the orderly and law abiding manner with which the elections were conducted."[5] He also affirmed that the voting showed "harmony and mutual understanding" between mainlanders and Formosans.

Independent reports are not yet available to confirm whether or not the Taiwanese are as enthusiastic about

4. H. Y. Moh, "New Deal for Taiwan," *Modern China*, October 1950, p. 32.
5. Chinese News Service, Press Release, February 20, 1951, p. 2.

this new development in self-government as the Taipei authorities maintain. It is clear that the newly-elected mayors and magistrates do not have full authority in local affairs since, under the Chinese Constitution, they may exercise only those powers delegated to them by the central authorities. Their powers are also shared with local officials appointed from above. In the case of Taipei municipality, Wu San-lien, a mainland Formosan who had been mayor of the city by appointment, resigned before the election in order to qualify. He won the contest at the polls and was subsequently named by the provincial government as concurrently head of the municipality.

That the Taiwanese are making headway toward local political responsibility is clear. Whether they are moving as fast as they would like and whether the personnel and political policies of the central administration are satisfactory to the people of Formosa is a question which cannot be conclusively answered.

Formosan Factions

Throughout its history the people of Formosa have experienced great difficulty in maintaining a united front against external powers, whether Dutch, Manchu or Japanese. Internecine rivalries have made it possible for the outsiders to play one faction against another in order to make their control secure. A similar situation prevails at the present time.

Three major tendencies may be noted among Formosan leaders, each of which may be further subdivided into different cliques. These groups include first, those who favor cooperation with the Kuomintang government; second, those who favor the Chinese Communists; and, third, the separatists who demand complete autonomy for the island.

The first group has been growing in strength as more

and more Formosans have been absorbed into the government. Some may collaborate for purely opportunistic reasons, others because they believe this course the best way to improve the lot of their compatriots in view of a situation which offers little prospect of establishing true independence.

The Communists

The Communists on Taiwan were never strong. Under the Japanese rule they associated themselves with the Japanese Communist Party. They were severely persecuted by the Imperial police, however, and their chief leaders spent many years in prison. After VJ-Day the leading Formosan Communist in Japan, Yang Chun-sung, remained active among Formosan residents of Japan. Following the victory of the Chinese Communists on the mainland, a growing number of Formosans in Japan, including a few wealthy men, gravitated toward the Communist group.

The Communists on Formosa itself encountered increasing difficulties after the February 28, 1947 incident and a number of them escaped to Hongkong in the fall of 1947. There, in collaboration with the anti-Kuomintang Democratic League, they organized a Formosan League for Democratic Self-Government. Under the editorship of Su Hsin they published pro-Communist, anti-Kuomintang and anti-American pamphlets. After the Chinese Communists gained control of Peking, Tientsin and Shanghai, a number of the Hongkong leaders went to these cities, where they began to play an active role in the new regime, especially in carrying on propaganda among Formosans resident on the mainland. A group of young Formosans who had been conscripted first by the Japanese and later by the Kuomintang were recruited for a special program at Hsinchuang, south of Shanghai, where they received preparatory training for taking over administrative posts in Formosa.

When the Communist East China Political and Military Council was organized in Shanghai, responsible for the administration of an area defined to include Taiwan, two Formosan Communists were made members of the group with responsibility for political work on the island. One of these was Tsai Chien, who had gone to the mainland early in the 1920's, had joined the Communist Party and played a role in the Kiangsi Soviet. He accompanied Mao Tse-tung on his Long March to Yenan and became a member of the party's Central Executive Committee.

The other was Miss Hsieh Hsueh-hung, who had been conspicuous during the February 28 incident, when she had been leader of a women's association in Taichung, central Formosa. Following the suppression of the uprising, Miss Hsieh led a group into the mountains, where she hoped to organize a guerrilla base. Conditions soon became too arduous for her, however, and she escaped to Hongkong, where she helped organize the Democratic Self-Government League. Subsequently she went to Peking to assume the vice chairmanship of the China Youth League and become a delegate to the Political Consultative Conference.

On Formosa itself the Communists have been active, especially in the distribution of handbills and posters. According to Nationalist reports, however, most Communist agents on the island are mainlanders rather than Formosans, and they concentrate their efforts on propaganda work among fellow exiles rather than among the local population. It is said that Communist agents receive salaries equivalent to twice that of a department head in the provincial administration. They appear to have established cells throughout the government services and focus their energies upon espionage and sabotage activities.

It is impossible to determine the attitude of the average Formosan toward the Communists. It is probable that in 1947 and 1948, when Kuomintang abuses were most serious and Communist promises appeared most attractive, the Formosans would have obstructed Nationalist attempts to defend the island in the event of a Communist bid for power. By 1951, however, reports of unsatisfactory conditions on the mainland combined with improvements at home may have caused politically articulate Formosans to change their minds.

The Separatists

Many Formosans no doubt felt the greatest amount of sympathy for those of their leaders who adopted a third point of view—opposition to both Communists and Nationalists. These leaders, however, after the events of 1947, were pretty largely forced into exile—at first in Shanghai, then, after the advent of the Communists, largely in Hongkong and Tokyo. Initially they demanded full independence. Later, as they realized their own helplessness, they turned more and more to the United States and the United Nations, seeking a plebiscite or a temporary UN trusteeship as a means of attaining autonomy for their island. Some of the outstanding leaders of this group were killed during and following the February 28 incident. Others, including Joshua and Thomas Liao, Peter K. Huang, Y. T. Tsong, and Frank S. Lim, have carried on their activities in exile.[6]

6. A manifesto demanding independence and a plebiscite was issued in Tokyo on August 23, 1948. It was signed by the following: Thomas Liao, Formosan League for Re-emancipation; Y. T. Tsong, League for Independence; S. L. Poan, League of Natives; Peter K. Huang, Youth League; K. C. Young, Demo-

Various efforts were made by these groups to form a stronger organization with a more coherent program. In May, 1950, a Formosan Democratic Independence Party was organized in Tokyo, including among its leaders General Wilfred Wong, James H. Chen, Gordon Tan, Y. T. Tsong and Frank Lim.

As these developments were taking place, there simultaneously emerged a number of Chinese political movements hoping to form a Third Force which would oppose both the Kuomintang and the Communists. In Hongkong, for example, partisans of Li Tsung-jen, the one-time Acting President of China, headed by former Legislative Yuan President Tung Kwan-hsien, organized a Democratic Progressive Party which also absorbed a number of local splinter groups. Leaders of this party then proposed an amalgamation of forces with the Formosan independence movement, promising Taiwan full autonomy should they succeed in establishing a new Chinese regime. The Formosan leaders responded by demanding the immediate organization of a provisional Formosan Free State government pending the Japanese peace conference and the subsequent holding of a plebiscite in Formosa itself.

Meanwhile Formosans both at home and in exile are confidently predicting that as the older Kuomintang leadership dies, younger Formosans will of necessity have to assume posts of responsibility. In December 1950 the Taiwan PPC formally demanded the election in 1951 of a Formosan governor for the island. If the Communists can be prevented from taking control of the island, the lines of distinction between mainland Nationalists and Formo-

---

cratic Reconstruction Association; Mrs. S. L. Chao, New Formosan Women's Association; Frank S. Lim, Students' League; K. K. Lim, Economic Research League; P. L. Khu, Literary Association; and G. T. Tang, People's League.

sans may gradually become blurred and disappear. If this happens, it may be anticipated that the collaborating Formosans at home and the exiled patriots will submerge their differences, especially as they begin to realize that there is no way to eliminate the power of the Nationalists on the island except through the intervention of a stronger external power.

On a less visionary plane, the Kuomintang government itself has made belated, though still inconclusive, efforts to reform the political basis of its own power and to win the support of the Formosan people. Whether or not it can be successful in the long run depends as much on its success in dealing with social and economic problems as on the formal political and governmental policies it adopts.

PART THREE

ECONOMIC

CHAPTER FIVE

Rice Basket and Arsenal

It is apparent that the ability of the Nationalists to maintain themselves on the island, to say nothing of ever being able to stage a comeback on the mainland, depends upon their capacity to satisfy their own material needs and those of the island's indigenous population. The quality of their achievement in this regard will determine, in large part, the extent to which the Formosans will support or hamper the efforts of the Kuomintang leaders. Ultimately, if the Nationalists are ever to cross the channel, it will be not only because of widespread Chinese dissatisfaction with the Communist regime but also because Nationalist achievements in Taiwan offer hope to mainland resistance leaders that a resurgent Kuomintang would meet the problems of China more competently than it did before 1949.

With a total area of 13,836 square miles, less than one-third the size of New York state, and a pre-war population of about 6 million (about 8 million in 1951),[1] approximately that of New York City (or Australia), it is apparent that Formosa's geographical resources are minute

1. The *China Handbook,* 1951, gives the population of Formosa in May 1950 as 7.6 million. An MSA report gives a figure of over 9.5 million in 1952. *U.S. Technical and Economic Assistance in the Far East* (Washington, Mutual Security Agency, March 1952), p. 12.

compared with those of China. Though completely lacking in iron ore deposits, it produced almost three million tons of coal in 1940 and is richly endowed for the production of hydroelectric power. It also has some gold, copper, silver and sulphur. Its major resource is its fertile land, with heavy, though variable, rainfall and a semi-tropical climate. Two-thirds of the area, however, consists of a forested mountain zone reaching, at its highest point, an elevation equivalent to that of the tallest peaks in the continental United States. Among the forests live the island's 150,000 aborigines. Only about one-fourth of the total area is cultivated, most of it in the western and northern coastal belt. The basic economy of the island, therefore, is agricultural, supplemented by the production of export crops and secondary manufacturing industries.

Development under the Japanese

During fifty years of Japanese occupation, the island's economy was developed as an integral part of the empire, providing raw and processed materials for consumption and further manufacture in the home islands and serving as a market for the products of Japanese industry. The Japanese stressed especially the cultivation of rice, which in 1940 provided 28.2 per cent of total exports, and sugar, which provided 41.5 per cent, virtually all of both exports being absorbed by Japan itself.

The development of rice culture—with three crops a year, intensive utilization of fertilizers and irrigation, and scientific techniques of breeding and processing—proved a great asset for both the people of Formosa and the Nationalist Government in that it provided the basic food requirements for the augmented population. The development of sugar culture, however, was less of an asset because production costs in Formosa are considerably higher than in other areas (such as Java). Thus Formosan cane fields produce only 60 per cent as much cane per acre as those of Java, where 12 to 14 months are necessary for the cane to mature as compared to 18 months in Taiwan. The Japanese themselves began to reduce sugar cultivation in Formosa after they occupied Indonesia and the Philippines. With the elimination of the special relationship to Japan, Formosa will find it increasingly difficult to sell sugar on the world market and will, consequently, be compelled to develop new industries and export commodities.

During the war the Japanese shifted important sectors of the Formosan economy to types of activity which would contribute to the war effort. Production equipment which had no immediate military use deteriorated for lack of adequate maintenance. During the last phases of the war, moreover, extensive damage to transportation and productive facilities was caused by Allied bombing. Thus the Formosan economy which was turned over to the Chinese at the end of the war, although far more developed industrially and agriculturally than the provinces of China Proper, had already suffered from a long-run distortion of its productive pattern and considerable short-run damage occasioned by the war.

Post-war Difficulties

The conditions of the post-war take-over greatly intensified these earlier difficulties. The Japanese policy of using their own nationals for all top positions in government and industry meant that few Formosans were prepared to assume executive responsibility. Similarly the Chinese, suddenly confronted with the task of taking over—or attempting to take over—the government of their own vast country, had very few surplus leaders qualified to direct an economic system as complex as that of Formosa. Those that might have been employed for this task, however, were not selected because the responsibility was given, for political reasons, to the war lord General Chen Yi and his personal entourage.

The Japanese technicians, who might have given invaluable assistance in the revival of Formosan production, were hastily evacuated to Japan, only a handful being permitted to remain as technical advisers. These few found that their presence was resented by both Formosans and Chinese, who were unwilling to appear to be in a position of subordination to Japanese; hence their advice was frequently disregarded. Before the war about 300,000 Japanese lived in Formosa. By June 1950 scarcely two dozen Japanese remained as employees of the Chinese administration. To make the situation worse, the Chen Yi regime, instead of utilizing Formosans wherever possible and advancing promising men into responsible positions, often displaced natives and substituted hangers-on from the mainland. Consequently, the already disorganized Formosan economy suffered even more acute distress.

Lack of technical personnel, however, was but one aspect of the tragedy of the Kuomintang's handling of its economic responsibilities in Taiwan. The Chen Yi administration was dominated by a "carpetbag" psychology. Unsure of their tenure and oriented basically to mainland conditions, the new rulers seemed concerned chiefly with extracting as rapidly as possible maximum profits with which to retire to the mainland. Nepotism, inefficiency and corruption brought the Formosan economy almost to the point of total collapse.

The basic aims of the Chen Yi regime were correlated with a lack of understanding of the necessity of stimulating productive processes. Instead, these mainland politicians were primarily interested in commercial and speculative transactions whereby quick profits could be made. The fact that the Shanghai market was starved for every sort of industrial and consumer goods meant that huge financial gains could be made through the sale of Formosan equipment and stocks. The result was a large-scale process of disinvestment in which the proceeds went, not into the government's budget for the provision of public services, but into the private vaults of individuals who were able to exploit their official positions for personal gain.

It was only natural that many Formosans, responding with intense hostility to the mainlanders, should attempt to sabotage and cheat their new rulers in retaliation for the disgraceful exploitation to which their land was being subjected. Their efforts intensified anti-Formosan sentiment on the part of the Chinese and further contributed to the breakdown of the Formosan economy.

Recent Improvements

Although some of the most conspicuous abuses were later curtailed under the administration of Governor Wei Tao-ming, the Chen Yi faction remained entrenched in the island's administrative apparatus. After General Chen Cheng took over the governorship, an attempt was made to strengthen the Formosan economy and restore production. Unfortunately the ingress from the mainland of a flood of civilian refugees, the remnants of the Nationalist army and staffs of central government offices caused further dislocations. Chinese workers and officials took over industrial and administrative positions *en masse* and many Formosans found it necessary to leave the major towns for their original village homes, where they contributed to rural unrest and imposed an added burden on the countryside.

With the appointment of K. C. Wu as governor, the establishment of the National Government in Taipei and the influx of American aid, a gradual improvement began to take place in the Formosan economic situation. Cut off from the mainland, the Kuomintang leaders began to interest themselves in the development of the island's productive capacity, while the Taiwanese themselves, recovering to some extent from the frustrations of the first postwar years and abandoning the expectation that some easy solution for their problems could be found, began to cooperate more effectively in tasks of rehabilitation. By 1950 production, especially of crops for domestic consumption, had fully recovered, although many export industries had failed to regain more than half of their pre-war standards. Meanwhile prices had achieved relative stability, although strong inflationary pressures continued and had begun to cause new price rises by early 1951. A turning point for the better, nevertheless, had definitely been passed by 1950 with the prospects for the future improved, though still unclear.

CHAPTER SIX

Agriculture, Forestry and Fisheries

In analyzing the economic situation in Formosa, attention may well be given first to the underlying situation in agriculture, the foundation upon which the rest of the economy is built. By 1940, under the intensive development spurred by the Japanese, about 2.1 million acres of land in Formosa were cultivated, of which 1.3 million were in rice and the remaining 0.8 million in other crops. Considerably more than half of this land was under irrigation.

Basic Conditions

The farming population in 1938, comprising 50 per cent of the island's total population, consisted of almost three million individuals, or 430,000 households. One-third of the farming population owned all the land it cultivated, the remaining two-thirds renting some land. However, only 36 per cent rented all the land it farmed, an intermediate group, about 31 per cent, consisting of farmers who owned some land and rented additional plots. Of the total arable land, 56.3 per cent was cultivated by tenants and 43.7 per cent by owners.

The largest landholder was the Japanese-owned Taiwan Development Company, which held 230,000 acres, property which was nationalized by the Chinese under the

Land Administration Bureau and rented out to tenants. Most of the landlords were native Formosans, though only one held an estate over 500 acres in size. That one died in 1946 and his lands were subdivided and distributed.

Of all farms in 1939, one-fourth were less than 1.2 acres in size, one-fifth were between 1.2 and 2.4 acres, while another one-fourth were between 2.4 and 4.8 acres in size. Only 0.12 per cent of the farms exceeded 48 acres. Since many of the farmsteads were owned by landlords who rented them to tenant farmers, it is clear that a relatively small number of owners held a disproportionately large amount of land, but authoritative figures on such holdings do not appear to be available.[1]

With regard to the rate of rents charged on the island, the figure of 53.9 per cent of the total main crops has been given by Kuomintang official sources as the average rental. The rate varied, however, from district to district, ranging from averages around 46 per cent in some localities to more than 62 per cent in others. It should be noted, however, that, in accordance with Chinese custom, rents were always determined by the output of main crops; subsidiary crops, such as vegetables, were not subject to taxation.

1. Although the source of the data is not given and the accuracy of the figures may be questioned, it may be of interest to cite the account given by a Russian writer, B. Alexandrov, in *Pravda* for January 13, 1951, in an article entitled "The Island of Taiwan" (*Soviet Press Translations*, February 15, 1951, p. 71). He maintains that 0.5 per cent of the proprietors—big landlords and agricultural companies—owned one-fourth of all arable land. This doubtless refers, in large part, to the extensive properties of the Japanese semi-official Taiwan Development Corporation, subsequently nationalized by the Kuomintang. Alexandrov also alleges that 43 per cent of the peasants held small farms averaging only 0.6 acres each. In interpreting this report, allowance, of course, should be made for the author's effort to depict the agrarian situation in the worst possible light.

FORMOSA: AGRICULTURAL PRODUCTION STATISTICS

	Pre-war	1945	1946	1947	1948	1949	1950
Rice							
Area (thousand hectares)	625[2]	510	564	678	718	748	781[4]
Production (thousand metric tons)	1,400	640	890	1,000	1,070	1,210	1,400[4]
Fertilizer used (thousand metric tons)	389	2	–	–	–	–	335
Yield (kilograms per hectare)	2,219	1,145	–	–	–	1,624	1,801
Sugar cane							
Area (thousand hectares)	162[1]	108	36	30	85	105	97
Production (thousand metric tons)	12,800	4,160	1,000	796	6,190	5,267	–
Yield (metric tons per hectare)	79	39	28	27	51	51	–
Sugar refined (thousand metric tons)	1,374[2]	86	31	263	634	612	350[4]
Sweet potatoes							
Area (thousand hectares)	139[1]	135	176	214	236	250	–
Production (thousand metric tons)	1,770	1,165	1,330	1,780	2,000	2,166	2,350
Wheat							
Area (thousand hectares)	10.5[1]	2.5	2.0	5.5	9.0	13.9	18.1
Production (thousand metric tons)	6.6	0.8	1.3	4.3	6.5	10.1	21.3
Tea							
Area (thousand hectares)	42.5[3]	23.6	23.8	31.7	33.0	36.0	35.1
Production (thousand metric tons)	14.0	1.4	2.9	7.4	8.5	10.2	10.7[4]
Peanuts							
Production (thousand metric tons)	31.7[1]	11.6	–	–	–	–	65?
Irrigated land (thousand hectares)	–	562	568	574	580	600	612

[1] 1937. [2] 1938. [3] 1939. [4] Estimate.
Source: Chiefly Han Lih-wu, *Taiwan Today.*

In October 1945, when the Chinese took over Formosa, the area of land under cultivation had fallen from 2.1 to 1.78 million acres. Moreover, the productivity of cultivated land had greatly declined. Three factors were chiefly responsible: first, the lack of fertilizer, previously imported from Japan, reduced yield per acre; second, disruption of irrigation works because of suspension of maintenance, coupled with storm and flood damage, cut into production; and third, some land was withheld from production to provide space for war-time airfields and related facilities. This latter land, amounting to about 238,500 acres, continued throughout the post-war years to be a bone of contention as the Chinese regime retained it for military purposes even though most of it was not actively in use.

The Taipei government has attempted to deal with these obstacles to production, claiming great success. The Formosan autonomist leaders have belittled the claims of the Kuomintang spokesmen, insisting that corresponding evils have attended apparent improvements. Doubtless the truth lies somewhere between these conflicting claims.

Rice Production

The position of rice production may be considered as a crucial test. The rice crop in 1938 was 1.4 million tons.[2] By contrast the 1945 crop was only 0.64 million tons. By 1949, however, production had risen to 1.2 million tons, to 1.48 million in 1951 and to an expected 1.6 million tons in 1952.

The original decline reflected a reduction in rice acreage to 1.2 million, a drop of 100,000 to 200,000 acres. But in 1950 an estimated 1.9 million acres was planted to rice. This made possible a crop slightly in excess of the Japanese record. However, it must be borne in mind that

2. All tonnage figures in this volume are in metric tons.

the additional 0.6 million acres represented a drastic sac-
rifice of other crops which might have been planted in
place of rice. Moreover, the population as a whole had
increased from about 6 million to almost 8 million so that
per capita production declined. If consumption levels were
to equal pre-war standards, the surplus available for export would be greatly curtailed. In 1940 the Japanese
could export more than 50 per cent of the Taiwan rice
crop. In 1950 only 15 per cent, about 200,000 tons, could
be shipped abroad.[3]

A second factor responsible for the increase in rice production was the application of fertilizer. In 1938 a total
of 389,300 tons of fertilizer had been used on rice fields.
In 1945 the amount had fallen to 1,960 tons. In 1950 a
total of 235,000 tons of fertilizer was used, making a major
contribution to increased productivity. The ECA played
a large role in this program, providing 140,000 tons as of
October 1950. By the end of 1951 ECA had paid for more
than $40 million worth of fertilizer. As a result about
280,000 tons of fertilizer were distributed during 1951,
and the goal for 1952 is 375,000 tons.

This fertilizer was sold to the farmers on the basis of
an exchange for rice. In this connection the Formosan
autonomist leaders complained that the exchange ratio
was unfair. Thus in 1949 the market price of fertilizer was
the equivalent of $70 per ton and that of rice $170, or 2.43
tons of fertilizer for one of rice. Nevertheless the Kuomintang agency, which had a monopoly of fertilizer distribution, would exchange only one ton of fertilizer for 1.5 or

3. According to official estimates, 1.21 million tons would be neces-
    sary to feed Formosa in 1950 on the basis of 288 pounds a year
    per person for 7,100,000 natives of Formosa, 440 pounds a year
    for 500,000 Chinese mainlanders, and 647 pounds a year for
    500,000 members of the armed forces. Han Lih-wu, *Taiwan
    Today* (Taipei, Hwa Kuo Publishing Co., 1951), p. 80.

more tons of rice. Thus 120,000 tons of fertilizer were distributed in exchange for about 180,000 tons of rice, whereas 50,000 tons of rice should have been enough to pay for the fertilizer.

Subsequently the ratio was revised so as to be more favorable to the farmer—1 ton of fertilizer to 1.3 of rice for the first crop in 1950, 1 to 1 for the second crop—but the rate apparently still did not correspond to relative market values. As a further safeguard an ECA agency, the (Sino-American) Joint Commission on Rural Reconstruction (JCRR), now supervises and inspects the distribution of fertilizer, utilizing 341 farmers' associations as well as the provincial government's food bureau and communications department.

The comparative efficiency of rice culture may be gauged from the fact that pre-war yield was 2,219 kilograms per hectare, as compared with 1,145 kilograms in 1945 when fertilizer distribution was almost nonexistent, and 1,801 kilograms per hectare in 1950 when fertilizer utilization, though not on the pre-war scale, had been revived.

Agrarian Reforms

As a further step toward the improvement of agricultural conditions, in 1949 the government under General Chen Cheng embarked on a program of rent reduction in accordance with an old Kuomintang law which had never been enforced. This law limited maximum rent to 37.5 per cent of the total main crops, an overall average reduction of 16.4 per cent of previous rent rates.[4] The JCRR has given its cooperation in the implementation of this

4. The basis of rent assessment is not the actual crop each year but, in accordance with ancient Chinese custom, an assigned quota for each field. The quota is based on a land survey made dur-

law. In June 1951 this provincial reform program was given new emphasis when it was promulgated as national law for future enforcement on the mainland.

The Formosan critics of this measure charge that it was largely undertaken to make the native landlords the scapegoats for the abuses perpetrated by the ruling mainland Chinese—it was easy for the Kuomintang to claim credit for a reform carried out at someone else's expense. Moreover, they maintain that the Kuomintang, by its fertilizer exchange program and by compelling farmers to sell all "surplus" rice at low fixed rates, actually deprived poorer peasants of all they had supposedly gained from the rent reduction. If all rice farmers had been tenants, then the gain for them from rent reduction in 1949 would have been 16.4 per cent of 1.2 million tons or about 200,000 tons. Since only about 61 per cent of the rice land was farmed by tenants, their net gain could have been only about 120,000 tons. This was roughly equivalent to what the government made in profit on its fertilizer exchange program.

In this connection it should also be noted that one-fourth of all tenants paid rent to the government, which owns almost 600,000 acres of arable land. Since the moun-

---

ing the latter part of 1950. In each county the land is graded according to a scale ranging from the most productive to the least productive land. The number of catties per hectare to be expected on each grade of land is determined and the 35.7 per cent rent fixed accordingly. Farmers who produce more than the assigned standard may keep the excess. It is not clear whether, in practice, rent would be reduced should production fall below the quota. Rents apply, of course, only to the main, not to subsidiary crops. It is interesting to note that the Communists in mainland China appear to be using the same quota system for the determination of taxes except that the rates are supposed to be substantially higher for rich peasants than for poor.

tain-forest areas are largely government-owned, 72 per cent of the island's surface is public land. However, government-held arable land totals only 6.65 per cent of the island's area. Of this amount, 209,143 acres were rented out to 107,671 tenants in 1948 at a rate, according to a report by Governor Wei in 1948, of 25 per cent. It may be noted that public arable land constitutes about one-fourth of all arable land, but that half of it is not cultivated.

Formosan reformers have advocated that the government turn over much of this land, especially the unused airfields, for crops, and that the rented land be made available for full ownership by native peasants. Instead, on a number of occasions the government has put land up for sale at prices which could be paid only by wealthy mainlanders. However, during the last two years 6,000 farm householders purchased 7,500 acres of land, according to a report by Nationalist Minister Tung Wen-chi in March 1951.[5] It is not clear how much of this was public land. Even if all of it was, it would have been only 0.014 per cent of the government-owned arable land. In January 1951 the administration took a step to meet these criticisms by announcing that 90,000 acres of vacant public land would be offered for sale to qualified tenant farmers on a ten-year instalment basis. The annual instalment, including taxes, is not to exceed 37.5 per cent of the main crop on the new land. It is too early yet to evaluate the success of this scheme, heralded as the first part of a new program to sell public land.

The government has been hopeful about the results of the rent reform, claiming that farmers have spent one-fourth of their additional income on increased food consumption and the rest for fertilizer, cattle, implements and other capital improvements.

5. Chinese News Service, Press Release, March 27, 1951.

In addition to the rent reduction feature, the government program, conducted with the strong cooperation of JCRR, has included: three to six year written leases in place of verbal agreements which could be terminated at any time by the landlord; substitution of direct leases between tenants and landlords for subleases made through land agents; the banning of advance deposits equivalent to a year's rent; reduction of rent in bad harvest years; prohibition of advance collection of rent; and complete elimination of rentals on subsidiary crops. If honestly and efficiently carried out, it is probable that a program of this character would win support from tenant farmers. Dr. Wolf I. Ladejinsky, American government land expert, after making a nine-week visit to Taiwan in 1951, noted a general improvement in rural conditions as compared with his earlier observations in 1949.[6]

Irrigation

Besides the use of fertilizer and changes in land tenure, rice production has been affected by the condition of the irrigation system. Before the war 60 per cent of Taiwan's arable land, 1.4 million acres, had been irrigated. Extensive war-time damage and neglect had reduced this system by 1945. However, according to Nationalist claims, by 1950 the total irrigated area had been increased to 1.5 million acres and repairs had been carried out over irrigation works serving a total area of 1.65 million acres.

In connection with irrigation projects JCRR has played an important role by providing about half the funds for the construction of dams and other waterworks. JCRR engineers consult with the Provincial Water Conservancy Bureau in selecting irrigation projects, notably those in

6. *Foreign Agriculture,* June 1950, pp. 130-35; also Chinese News Service, Press Release, July 10, 1951, p. 3.

which the greatest immediate results can be achieved for the least expense, and then inspect construction and make payments in accordance with the progress of the work. Formosan critics insist that the Nationalists have lagged in maintaining the irrigation system, but it appears that real progress in this field has recently been made.

Another factor responsible for the relative increase in total rice production was the introduction of improved seed—under the aegis of JCRR—which was planted on 30 per cent of the total rice acreage. ECA has estimated that its irrigation and seed improvement projects together brought an increase in the rice crop of 30,000 tons in 1950. At world prices this was worth about $4.2 million, or twice the entire amount allocated for the JCRR program. Nevertheless it accounted for only about 2 per cent of the year's total crop of 1.4 million metric tons. Thus while the JCRR operations clearly more than paid for themselves, they by no means provided an easy way of solving the island's food problems.

Other Food Crops

With regard to other crops besides rice, it may be said in general that the Formosans have expanded the production of food for domestic consumption, even considerably above pre-war levels, but the output of commercial crops used chiefly for export has not recovered to former levels. For example, sweet potatoes, used not only for human consumption, but also as hog and cattle feed and in the production of starch and alcohol, reached the level of 2.36 million tons in 1951 as compared with peak pre-war production of 1.77 million achieved in 1937, and a level of 1.17 million tons in 1945. This crop grows well on marginal, sandy soils found in western Taiwan. The area devoted to its cultivation increased from 333,000 acres in

1945 to almost 618,000 acres in 1950. Since the 1950 crop fully met domestic demand and there is little possibility of export, it is likely that production of sweet potatoes will not be further expanded.

Domestic requirements of wheat are estimated at about 70,000 tons a year, a great increase over pre-war requirements because of the large influx of wheat-eating mainland Northerners. Since wheat may be planted between the second and the first crops of rice and as a winter catch crop, it should be possible to expand its culture considerably. Nevertheless, insular production in 1950 was only 21,300 tons, or less than one-third of domestic requirements. This represented a vast proportional increase over the 750 tons produced in 1945, however, and more than three times the former peak production of 6,600 tons in 1941. Acreage also expanded from less than 5,000 in 1946 to almost 45,000 acres in 1950. To make up the deficiency, ECA financed the import of more than 9,000 tons of wheat and flour in 1950. Existing flour mill capacity can take care of about 25,000 tons a year. Since the farmers keep about half of their wheat production to feed livestock, it will be necessary for Taiwan to continue importing more than 20,000 tons of wheat a year. In addition, the import of more than 40,000 tons of flour annually would be necessary to make up the needs of the market.

Another crop which has expanded under the impact of strong domestic demand is peanuts, which reached an estimated 65,000 tons in 1950 as compared with the post-war low of 11,560 tons and a pre-war level of 31,700. Nevertheless, peanut production failed to catch up with requirements for home consumption and the ECA included about 1,000 tons of peanuts among its 1950 imports. In addition, as another major source of edible oils, protein and animal feed, ECA paid for the import during 1950 of more than 18,000 tons of soya beans.

Other Export Crops

In contrast to these food crops, those produced for export have failed notably. Partly this has been the normal result of the disruption of trade with Japan and the initial substitution of the feverish and unhealthy Shanghai commerce, which depended on a process of disinvestment rather than sale of items from current production. As trade relations with Japan have been gradually restored, it may be expected that demand for, and consequently production of, former export items will be stepped up. During the fiscal year ending June 30, 1950 trade between Japan and Formosa was valued at $56 million. During September 1950 a trade pact was signed between Taipei and the US Occupation authorities in Tokyo under which commerce on the order of $200 million was expected for the year 1950–51. This pact has been extended on an annual basis pending conclusion of a new general trade treaty.

The largest item in pre-war trade, as noted above, was sugar, which went almost exclusively to Japan. At peak levels in 1938–39, over 391,000 acres were planted to this crop, producing 12.8 million tons of cane. By 1946 cane acreage had fallen to less than 74,000, with production at the 0.8 million ton level. By virtue of a strong campaign organized by the Taiwan Sugar Corporation, the Nationalist-controlled body which had taken over Japanese-operated sugar refineries, acreage in 1949–50 reached more than 259,000. Production, however, amounted to less than 5.3 million tons, representing an output of less than half the pre-war level and a yield of only 20 tons per acre compared with the Japanese standard of 33. Despite this, sugar in 1950 played more than twice as important a role in Formosan trade as it did in 1940, accounting for over 85 per cent of total exports, thus reflecting the even more drastic decline of other exports.

Formosan sugar benefits from the fact that its purchase does not require dollars, and may therefore be more readily acquired by dollar-short countries, such as Japan and Great Britain. The demand for Formosan sugar is also influenced by such extraneous factors as the volume of Cuban sugar purchases by the United States. The greater such buying in any year, the less the rest of the world may obtain from Cuba and the more it must depend on secondary sources such as Formosa. Taiwan sugar cannot be sold directly in the American market because its color does not meet the prescribed standards. In the long run, therefore, Formosan sugar has a precarious place on the world market, and undue dependence on this export crop is dangerous for the future of the island's economy. Since the curtailment of sugar acreage has resulted largely from the need to increase rice acreage, it is difficult to see how Formosa can greatly expand the production of any other commercial crop without cutting into essential food culture.

The third most valuable pre-war export crop was the annual sale of 135,000 tons of bananas, accounting for about 3 per cent of the value of all exports. Total production of bananas in 1937 amounted to 218,600 tons, but the post-war crop fell to 32,000 tons. Acreage had declined from 52,400 to 14,000. As the Japanese market revives, production should recover. By 1950 over 42,000 acres were cultivated, yielding a total of almost 120,000 tons.

Pineapples constituted another important item in Formosa's pre-war exports, valued at 2.3 per cent of the total. Peak production under the Japanese was 145,800 tons. In

1945 output fell to 17,500 tons, and by 1950 this crop had regained less than a third of its former level with an output of 42,000 tons. Since pineapples can be grown on hillsides unsuited to the culture of staple crops, it is estimated that the acreage of 12,800 planted in 1950 could readily be expanded to over 74,000. Under the Japanese 25,700 acres had been used for pineapples.

According to a five-year production plan for pineapples announced by the Nationalist Government, 300,000 cases of canned fruit were expected in 1951, with the production goal to be increased to 450,000 in 1953 and 660,000 by 1955. Since the 1950 crop was equivalent to about 90,000 cases, this program represented an ambitious development plan. Advance reports indicated that the first year goal might be attained.[7]

Among the better known Formosan exports was tea. The Oolong, or half fermented, product was largely sold to the United States before the first World War. Pouchong, a slightly fermented tea, subsequently became more important as an export to China and southeast Asia. Black, or totally fermented, tea has found increasing markets during the last fifteen years and green, or unfermented, tea has, since the war, been exported to China, North Africa and South America. Pre-war production reached a peak of 14,000 tons making use of 104,000 acres. Post-war output collapsed to 1,430 tons with an acreage of 58,000. Subsequently production gradually increased, reaching 10,100 tons in 1949 with 89,000 acres in tea. The closing of the Chinese market and competition in southeast Asia (caused by tea-dumping by the Communists utilizing captured stocks) dealt the industry a severe blow in 1950, when production declined to 8,000 tons. Nevertheless, this product held third place among export items.

7. Chinese News Service, Press Release, August 7, 1951, p. 3.

Forest Products

One of Formosa's greatest natural resources is the forest cover which clothes two-thirds of the island, providing an estimated standing timber reserve of 7.3 billion cubic feet. The great bulk of this, however, is located on the inner mountains ranging from 7,000 to 12,000 feet above sea level and cannot be commercially exploited without extensive capital investment. The Japanese had built railway lines and installed equipment for logging on three mountains. Vegetation ranges from the subtropical forests of the foothills, with bamboo groves and giant camphor trees, through coniferous forests in the intermediate zone to an alpine cover on the highest peaks. The Japanese government attempted to conserve the natural cover over much of the mountain area both to prevent floods and to lay the foundation for hydroelectric development.

The forests also provided home reserves for the aboriginal population, which numbered between 150,000 and 200,000. The Japanese have a tradition of caring for forest lands which was early applied to Formosa with the development of fire control measures and programs of reforestation and prevention of soil erosion. This contrasted with the customary practices of the Taiwanese, who, like the Chinese from whom they descended, had different views on conservation, and often burned forest cover as a means of clearing land or driving the aborigines back into the mountains.

After the war it became clear that the Japanese had failed to educate the Formosan population as a whole to understand the value of their conservation measures, which had often been carried out under duress. As a result peasants frequently cut nearby trees for fuel or construction without regard to the consequences for embankments and flood control, to say nothing of irrigation, which directly affected their own welfare. When the Nationalist administration established itself, a virtual government monopoly was formed by taking over Japanese operations. Logging, however, was conducted in a most wasteful way without regard for replanting. Thus was compounded damage to the forests which had already been begun during the war period when the Japanese themselves, under military pressure, permitted reduction of forest areas to meet emergency needs.

Since 1948, according to the official program, timber removal is being restricted to the rate of new planting and profits from government logging operations are designated for reforestation purposes. It is said that by 1949 more than 36,000 acres were replanted with trees. Figures on post-war lumbering operations are not available.

One variety of tree which yields a product of exceptional interest is the camphor, in which Formosa holds a pre-eminent position as the world's main source, producing about 3,000 tons annually before the war, or 95 per cent of the world total. The camphor tree requires at least sixty years of growth before it becomes economically valuable. The Japanese relied on wild growth and also stimulated the planting of new trees. Past practice was for the trees to be cut into chips and the oil and crystals distilled from steam rising over vats in which the wood was boiled. About one pound of crystals and four ounces of oil could be obtained from fifty pounds of chips. This oil was then sold, through agencies, to the government monopoly which handled further processing and sales.

With the development of synthetic camphor in the United States and Germany, the price fell and the Formosan industry necessarily declined while the Japanese searched for alternative ways of capitalizing on their unique resource. Meanwhile extensive stocks accumulated. After the war these were expropriated by the Chinese and promptly sold. It is not surprising therefore that, as Dr. Han asserts, 1945 was the "best year for camphor production," with the output of refined camphor, at 812 tons, exceeding peak production in Japanese times.[8] In 1949 an improved refining process was developed which may bring about a revival of this industry. Exports of the refined product, in any case, rose from 588 tons in 1949 to 996 tons in the first half of 1950.

Fisheries

A major source of food supply for Taiwan consists of fish taken from the deep ocean, coastal and inland waters, and homestead ponds where peasants breed their own fish. The Japanese had developed ocean fishing until it became the largest component of the marine industry, utilizing 149 vessels by 1940, when the peak catch of 57,000 tons was recorded. During the war the fishing fleet was decimated so that in 1945, with 46 largely crippled ships, the Chinese were able to bring in only 68 tons. In the last few years, however, attention has been given to improving this industry. With 72 vessels in operation by 1950, the catch for January through August reached the figure of 8,888 tons. Late in July 1951 the first entirely Chinese-constructed diesel-powered fishing craft—a 90 by 15½ foot, 78-ton refrigerated vessel—was launched, and a second was nearing completion. American aid has also been given to the restoration of this industry.

In contrast to deep sea fishing, which was introduced by the Japanese, the Formosans themselves had traditionally practiced domestic fish culture in ponds which also served other domestic purposes and even provided moat-like pro-

8. Han Lih-wu, *op. cit.*, p. 117.

tection for the farmstead. With the development of an adequate fish supply from commercial sources, this domestic culture declined, with production gradually falling during the pre-war years, from almost 18,000 tons in 1933 to 11,000 in 1941. After the war, with other sources of fish curtailed, domestic culture revived from a low of 5,000 tons in 1945 to 25,300 in 1948 and 16,300 for the period from January through August 1950.

Coastal fishing similarly declined from a peak of 29,300 tons in 1933 to less than 9,000 in 1945. This industry is largely carried on by farmers living along the coast, as an auxiliary occupation. Not being dependent on large vessels or complex equipment, this industry made a rapid recovery, achieving by 1948 the peak level of pre-war production. The experience of inland stream fishing was somewhat parallel to that of coastal fishing. The revival of domestic and coastal fishing as the more economic deep sea fishing declined may be judged from the fishing employment statistics. Whereas an average of only about 43,000 fishermen were employed in the pre-war years 1937–43, there were over 235,000 workers engaged in fishing in 1949—largely in the less productive ponds, streams and coastal waters.

In 1951 the National Government announced that 60 million new Taiwan yuan (about $430,000) would be made available in loans to fishermen to acquire needed equipment. A total catch for 1951 of 110,000 metric tons was hoped for.[9]

Livestock

Traditionally the value of livestock in the Formosan economy was second only to that of rice and sugar, accounting for 20 per cent of agricultural production. Un-

9. Chinese News Service, Press Release, August 14, 1951, p. 3.

like the latter, however, the products of animal husbandry were generally not exported but were used for domestic consumption, especially pork, the favorite meat among Chinese.

There was an average of 327 hogs per 1,000 persons on the island before the war, a total of 1.8 million according to the 1938 census. An average of one million hogs were slaughtered annually with consumption averaging twenty-five pounds per person. The Japanese introduced Berkshires, which constituted about 90 per cent of the herd at the outbreak of war. During the war the hog population declined, largely as a result of increasing military demand for leather and bristles as well as for meat. By 1945 only about half a million hogs remained. The Chinese, with some assistance from JCRR, have given considerable attention to the restoration of the hog population, and to a campaign against hog cholera and erysipelas. As a result by 1950 the number of hogs almost reached pre-war standards with a figure of 1.5 million.

The traditional draft animal used in Formosan, as in Chinese, rice culture is the water buffalo. The Japanese, to provide a better general draft animal and meat producer, had introduced some Indian humped cattle, from which a cross-breed of the native variety of cattle had been developed. In 1939 there were 260,000 buffalo and 65,000 "yellow cows," the cross-breed, on the island, a total of 325,000. This number had fallen to 291,000 by 1945 as a result of excessive war-time slaughtering. By 1950, however, the cattle population had climbed to 375,000, a figure still short of the half million needed for adequate cultivation and transportation. An epidemic of rinderpest broke out in October 1949 but, with timely aid from JCRR, was overcome with the loss of only 126 head of cattle.

The total poultry population of 9.5 million in 1938—including 7 million chickens, 2 million ducks, 400,000 geese and 35,000 turkeys—had declined to 7 million in 1945, but by 1950 had recovered to a level of more than 9.1 million.

The Japanese had tried before the war, with but little success, to establish silk production in Taiwan. During the last year JCRR has shown an interest in the possibilities of this industry and has allotted funds to the China Silk Corporation for use in developing Formosan sericulture. By introducing better varieties of worm, mulberry seedlings and improved techniques, production was increased several fold in a few months' time and a way of providing supplementary income for farmers demonstrated.

Joint Commission on Rural Reconstruction

One of the most notable features of the American aid program on Formosa has been the work of the Joint Commission on Rural Reconstruction. As a semi-autonomous body headed by a commission of five members, two American and three Chinese, with Dr. Chiang Mon-lin serving as chairman and including—until his recent resignation—Dr. Raymond T. Moyer, director of ECA's China mission, this organization has been in a unique position to influence favorably the development of Formosan agriculture. By December 31, 1950 JCRR had obligated the equivalent of $3.6 million, largely in local currency—the counterpart of ECA grants—for use in its program. Of this amount the largest item, $1.2 million, was for agricultural improvement and $0.9 million for irrigation.

A phase of the program which the commissioners have come to recognize as increasingly important is the development of a network of farmers' associations. These organizations were originally established by the Japanese with 341 township and almost 5,000 village chapters throughout the island. However, they had been largely utilized to maintain the political authority of the Japanese regime, as well as to provide certain rural services, such as the distribution of supplies, the extension of credit and cooperative buying. After the war a tendency developed for local landowners and merchants to take over control of these organizations. The JCRR has attempted to reorganize them as authentic, non-political organizations to serve the farmers' own interests. One means of doing this has been by the introduction of a system of electing association officials which is intended to ensure that only *bona fide* farmers are put in leadership positions. Among other duties farmers' associations are given primary responsibility for the enforcement of the rent reduction program. Rural home improvement and youth programs are also being developed in conjunction with the work of the associations. The associations are becoming the community centers for the farmers; they handle the distribution of chemical fertilizers and beancake, and provide other cooperative and credit facilities.

As a related activity, JCRR established a special research group to study marketing policies, to investigate rice production costs and crop reporting systems and to tackle the important question of rural credit.

In addition to its work of helping to finance irrigation and conservation work, JCRR has contributed toward the improvement of livestock, strengthened rural public health programs, supervised fertilizer distribution and carried out experiments in audio-visual education.

Some conception of the broad scope of the JCRR program and its relatively low cost may be gained from the following table:

Program	No. of projects in progress, 1950	Amount paid (thousand U.S. $)
Agricultural improvement ...	95	576
Farmers' organizations	8	166
Irrigation	20	198
Rural health	20	197
Land reform	7	54
Animal husbandry	18	316
Food and fertilizer	5	58
Information and education...	3	32
Administration—local costs ...		674
Administration— American staff		194
	176	2,465

Only the administrative costs of the American staff were paid for directly out of US-appropriated funds, the rest being derived from the local currency counterpart obtained from sales of ECA-financed imports.[10]

10. For more details see quarterly reports to Congress of ECA; *The Program of the JCRR*, published by ECA, no date; *General Report of the JCRR, October 1, 1948 to February 15, 1950* (Taipei, 1950); *U.S. Economic Assistance to Formosa*, 1 January to 31 December 1950 (Washington, ECA, 1951).

CHAPTER SEVEN

Industrial Development

Since Formosan industry had been largely developed or taken over by the Japanese, and since the Nationalists expropriated all Japanese property, it naturally followed that Taiwan industry has, to a large extent, come under government control. In the early days of Chen Yi's administration, committees were formed under government commissions, such as that for industry and mining. In due time these committees acquired semi-autonomous status and became known as corporations. Individual politicians appointed to direct these committees became, by the same process, heads of giant concerns in which the distinction between private and public interest became blurred. Finally, because of the great wealth and power—especially through concurrent control over licensing and other administrative policies—of these new companies, private Formosan concerns found it increasingly difficult to remain solvent and many were compelled to abandon their activities. Thus in large part the new concerns became semi-public and semi-private monopolies.

Public and Private Industry

Some of them, of course, are avowedly government monopolies, such as the Taiwan Tobacco and Wine Monopoly, the Taiwan Camphor Bureau, and the Chinese Salt Corporation. Others are virtual monopolies, in such fields as sugar, power, fertilizer, pulp and paper, petroleum and shipbuilding. At the other extreme there are fields in which production, largely for domestic consumption, had been developed and remains in the hands of Taiwanese. In rice milling, the manufacture of soap, vegetable oil, rubber shoes and tires, etc., small private concerns remain predominant, although even in these fields government concerns have intruded, as in the production of one-fourth of the soap. In some intermediate spheres, government and private production are more nearly balanced—70 per cent of coal output is privately produced, and 80 per cent of the printing. Private companies own 60,000 spindles as compared with 20,700 in the hands of public enterprise, but (as Dr. Han remarks) "only a small portion of the private is in actual operation." [1]

The value of public production in 1949 was estimated at 718 million new Taiwan yuan (about $70 million), as compared with private production variously given as between 400 and 814 million yuan. In terms of employment private industry was estimated to provide about 79,000 jobs as compared with 67,700 working for public enterprises. Approximately 60 per cent of the total output of private industry was in food processing, almost entirely rice milling. Over one-third of those working for private concerns were in small establishments employing less than ten workers.

Private concerns were predominantly small-scale domestic industries. Of 7,049 independent businesses listed in 1949, 4,456, or 63 per cent, employed less than five regular workers each, 1,282 employed 5 to 9 workers, 459 em-

1. Han Lih-wu, *Taiwan Today* (Taipei, Hwa Kuo Publishing Co., 1951), p. 121.

ployed 10 to 14, 519 employed between 15 and 29, and only 333 factories, or 4.7 per cent, hired more than 30 regular workers. More than half of these units consisted of small rice mills.

At the other extreme virtually all large factories have been consolidated under the control of eighteen public corporations classified into three main groups, the first under the authority of the National Resources Commission, the second under the provincial government and the third under joint operation by national and provincial authorities.[2]

Sugar Refining

The most important element in the Formosan industrial picture is undoubtedly the refining of sugar, which has been brought almost exclusively under the control of the Taiwan Sugar Corporation, and accounts for half of the total value of all production by public industries. The corporation provides employment, directly or indirectly, for approximately a million Taiwanese, and is thus one of the most powerful single influences in the island's life.

The corporation was formed to manage the properties

2. The eighteen corporations are the following: *National:* (1) Chinese Petroleum Corporation; (2) Taiwan Aluminum Works; (3) Taiwan Gold and Copper Mining Administration; (4) Chinese Salt Corporation; (5) Hsinchu Coal Mining Administration; (6) Taiwan Steel Works. *National-Provincial:* (7) Taiwan Power Co.; (8) Taiwan Sugar Corporation; (9) Taiwan Fertilizer Co.; (10) Taiwan Cement Corporation; (11) Taiwan Alkali Co.; (12) Taiwan Pulp and Paper Corporation; (13) Taiwan Shipbuilding Co.; (14) Taiwan Machinery Manufacturing Corporation. *Provincial:* (15) Taiwan Industry and Mining Corporation (an omnibus holding company for many subsidiaries); (16) Taiwan Camphor Bureau; (17) Taiwan Tobacco and Wine Monopoly; (18) Taiwan Agricultural and Forestry Development Corporation. Han Lih-wu, *op. cit.,* pp. 100-101.

of four Japanese sugar companies which operated forty-two factories. The plants had been severely damaged by air attacks because they produced industrial alcohol. In addition to refineries, the corporation owns 74,000 acres of plantations, 1,738 miles of light railways and about 400 miles of sidings. Peak output of the refineries before the war was 1.4 million tons. In the post-war chaos, output reached its nadir in 1946 with less than 31,000 tons. In 1948 it jumped to over 600,000 tons, a rate retained in 1949 but drastically reduced in 1950 by cutbacks in sugar planting, resulting in an output of about 350,000 tons, while production in 1951 is recorded as 354,000 tons.

Failure of the corporation to provide technical services to which sugar farmers had become accustomed under the Japanese was one important factor in the initial decline of sugar productivity. More important, however, was the low compensation paid to the farmers by the company, despite its own hectic profits. In an effort to expand sugar acreage, the corporation offered to pay each farmer half of the sugar extracted from his cane. The result was an immediate jump reflected in the 1948 figures. In practice, however, the farmers did not receive as much compensation as they had expected, which accounts for the large drop in the 1950 crop. The corporation reportedly calculated output on the basis of 10 per cent of the weight of the cane instead of 13 per cent, the figure employed by the Japanese, according to Joshua Liao. Moreover, only 20 per cent of the payment was actually made in sugar, the rest being made in cash, not according to the market price but according to a lower fixed rate. The farmers simply found it more profitable to put their land back into rice production. The loss of the mainland sugar market, entailing a drop in sugar prices, was another important factor helping to account for the decline in production.

To meet this situation the sugar corporation has promulgated a program calling for the introduction of a better variety of sugar cane, mechanization in sugar plantations, development of underground water for irrigation, and land reclamation. It is too early to predict whether this program will bring about the increased production that is hoped for.

Domestic requirements for sugar amount to about 50,000 tons a year, leaving the bulk of production for export. Between 1947 and 1949, 64.7 per cent of sugar exports went to Japan, 22.7 per cent to Great Britain, and 7.65 per cent to Hongkong. China might potentially develop into a sugar market but this is certainly not an immediate prospect. As noted above, undue reliance on the sugar industry has been a basic weakness of the Formosan economy. If production of other commodities could be expanded to take its place, the people of Taiwan would, in the long run, stand to gain.

Among other export industries may be mentioned the production of salt, which has kept up pre-war standards of about 200,000 tons a year. Since domestic demand amounts to only about 50,000 tons, the remainder is available for export, largely to Japan. Four Japanese concerns which produced various salt products were brought under the control of the government-operated Taiwan Alkali Company. Caustic soda, hydrochloric acid, liquid chlorine and bleaching powder are the main products, but output is limited chiefly by the market rather than plant capacity.

Coal Mining

With an estimated reserve of 420 million tons, coal production has been an important industry in Taiwan. Immediately after the war fantastic profits were made by selling the fuel in Shanghai. Pre-war average output was 1.5

million tons a year, with a peak of 2.8 million tons reached in 1940. Post-war production climbed from a low of 0.8 million tons in 1945 to 1.6 million by 1949, enough, apparently, to satisfy domestic demand. Except for the unusual post-war situation in Shanghai, Formosan coal does not appear to be a practicable export commodity. It is chiefly found in thin veins, and its production costs price it out of the world market.

After the war the Provincial Government's Commission of Industry and Mines took over Japanese concerns but found a great many independent Taiwanese-operated mines. There ensued a struggle in which the new government agency, according to Joshua Liao, attempted to establish a monopoly, first by confiscating the property of Taiwanese who could not prove their ownership—which was frequently the case—and then by obstructing the delivery of mine rehabilitation equipment provided by UNRRA. Finally many Formosan operators began to cease operations. The administration, realizing that this would curtail the sales in Shanghai, offered to split the profits with independent owners who would sign a contract to sell their production to the Department. After the contracts had been signed, however, the luckless operators found that their coal was resold at a nominal mark-up to the government's Taiwan Trading Bureau, which, in turn, sold in Shanghai at large profits to be shared among the officials involved.

Following the loss of Shanghai to the Communists, however, the government sold some sixty pits to private owners, as output thereafter could be sold only for domestic use. Subsequently government-owned mines produced only about 30 per cent of the island's total supply with the remainder coming from private pits.

Electric Power

Electrification of Taiwan had been extensively carried out by the Japanese, reaching every rural community and providing industrial power to a degree rare in Asia. Pre-war standards are indicated by an output of 1.2 billion kilowatt hours in 1943. War-time bombing damaged some of the main plants and a disastrous flood knocked out most of the generating capacity of the system serving the eastern part of the island, a system which remained in 1950 limited to a peak load of 3,000 kilowatts as compared with a former capacity of ten times as much.

Production in 1945 for the island as a whole amounted to 357,000 kilowatt hours. This decline, however, represented only in part damage to installations, for whereas the remaining plant facilities could generate 84,000 kilowatts, the peak load was only 53,700. Prices of available electricity were kept so high that they may have accounted for the bankruptcy of some small industries.

With the repair of generating facilities—three-fourths of which are operated by water power—and the introduction into Taiwan of electric equipment removed from the mainland before the advancing Communists, power production has steadily increased, reaching an estimated one billion kilowatt hours in 1950. ECA has authorized the expenditure of $5.2 million for power projects intended to further advance the provision of electric power, thus laying the foundation for expansion of Taiwan's industry. By May 1951 output in the island's western system had jumped to 192,000 kilowatts, exceeding the pre-war standard of 152,000. By the end of 1951, according to the development program mapped out by the J. G. White Engineering Corporation under an ECA contract, output should have reached the 240,000 kilowatt level.

Other Industries

One of the essential ingredients for the maintenance of agricultural productivity in Taiwan is fertilizer. As indicated above, 389 million metric tons were utilized for rice alone before the war. Most of this came from Japan and constituted Taiwan's largest single import item—exceeding 400,000 tons a year—although as a percentage of total imports it was not large. Domestic chemical fertilizer production totaled only 33,858 tons in 1939, but by 1945 it had dwindled to the zero point.

In order to help revive agriculture, the ECA gave first priority to fertilizer imports. By the end of 1950, ECA had authorized $17 million for this commodity, and by the end of 1951 over $40 million had been authorized for fertilizer —paying for more than 300,000 tons.

Meanwhile ECA also rendered assistance to Taipei in its program for expanding domestic fertilizer production, which grew to an estimated output of 55,000 tons in 1950. The island's two superphosphate plants have a capacity of 40,000 tons a year. By 1952 it is hoped to raise the figure to 116,000 tons. The whole program is under the control of the government's Taiwan Fertilizer Company.

Among other industries, the expansion of textile production is worthy of comment. With ECA assistance, the number of spindles was increased from 20,000 early in 1950 to 65,000 by the spring of 1951. Through domestic production of textiles ECA has hoped to reduce greatly one of the heavy drains on foreign exchange. Raw cotton imports, however, would continue to be necessary as domestic production amounted to only about 253 tons in 1950. This situation was reflected in ECA-financed shipments of cotton costing $1.06 million in 1949, and jumping to programmed expenditures of $18 million for raw

cotton by the end of 1951. The 1950 cotton imports paid
for by ECA amounted to 15,104 bales or 93 per cent of all
such imports during the year. This kept all usable spindles
in operation. When other spindles are put into operating
condition, and all existing mills attain maximum production levels, Taiwan may have an annual consumption requirement of 40,000 bales of cotton. The spinning and
weaving of this cotton should provide the major part of
the island's consumer needs for textiles.

Cement production rose from 22,000 tons in 1949 to
35,000 tons by 1951. ECA helped make this possible by
paying for the import during 1950 of over 5,000 tons of
gypsum, which is used in the proportion of 3.5 tons to
every 100 tons of cement. This was considered especially
important because of the need for concrete in highway
and port rehabilitation and in the construction of build-
ings, new factory installations, etc.

Another industry of peculiar significance to Formosa is
the local refining of petroleum products. Despite a fair
amount of exploratory activity, oil has not been found in
important quantities on the island. Nevertheless the exist-
ence of Japanese-built refineries (now owned by the Chinese Petroleum Corporation, a government agency), capable of processing 30,000 to 50,000 tons of crude oil per
month, is an important asset. To make possible utilization
of this resource, ECA financed during 1950 the import of
more than 72,000 tons of crude oil. It should become possible for Taiwan not only to refine the bulk of its own
local demand for petroleum products but even to produce
some for export.

Transport and Communications

The Japanese had developed in Taiwan an extensive
and well run railway system, which, in 1943, included 565

revenue miles. Although it deteriorated greatly after the war, repairs were made and by 1950 the full mileage had been restored and even added to. In 1950, after repairs, and with assistance valued at $3.9 million from ECA, there were in Formosa 188 serviceable locomotives as compared with 241 under the Japanese in 1944; 544 passenger coaches in service as compared with 506 in 1944; and 5,325 freight cars as compared with 5,804 in 1944. According to the Taiwan Railway, the daily average of passengers carried in 1950 was 187,905 as compared with 178,803 in 1944. In freight, however, a daily average of only 17,861 tons was carried in 1950 as compared with 24,650 in 1941. By early 1950, 435 trains were running daily as compared with 391 in 1941 and only 170 in 1946. Despite these records, the situation is not satisfactory since much of the rolling stock is over age and trackage has badly deteriorated. ECA has financed the purchase of bridge spans, steel rails, cross ties, telephone and copper wire, locomotive and car repair material, new passenger coaches, and other equipment needed to strengthen and improve the railway system. More than $1.5 million was spent for these supplies in 1950.

The extensive highway system built by the Japanese was allowed to disintegrate markedly both before and after the war's end. In the last few years, however, repairs have been widely made and the use of roads, especially for bus transportation, has been greatly expanded. ECA has contributed to the rehabilitation of the road system and is helping to build the Silo bridge across the Cho Shui Chi, which will link the northern and southern systems.

Similar achievements have been chalked up in the field of communications, with restoration of disrupted telephone and telegraph services. Taiwan's merchant shipping resources have been substantially increased by the acquisition of former mainland holdings plus vessels acquired from the United States. Deteriorated or destroyed harbor facilities have likewise been improved.

ECA Aid

The US Economic Cooperation Administration has been able to render signal services to the Taipei government in its efforts to rehabilitate Formosan industry. Working in conjunction with the ECA China Mission is a Chinese cabinet-level agency called the Council for United States Aid (CUSA). Meeting together the ECA and CUSA have established a Taiwan Joint Committee to plan the aid program. ECA has supplied capital equipment for the maintenance and rehabilitation of power, transportation and communications facilities and industries. It has also paid for the services of an American firm, the J. G. White Engineering Corporation, which has provided advisory facilities. The chief categories of aid financed and the amount authorized for each from June 5, 1950 through the end of 1951 are as follows (in millions): fertilizer, $40.9; fats and oils, $10.5; petroleum, $10.0; raw cotton, $18.1; textiles, $6.4; machinery and equipment, $9.7; wheat and flour, $9.4; iron and steel mill materials, $11.0; lumber, $2.7; and others, totaling $148.5 million.

As its program has gradually moved into full gear, ECA has made an ever larger contribution to the rehabilitation of the Formosan economy. During the whole period from 1945 to March 1950 ECA had spent only $2.3 million for the reconstruction of the island's electric power, railways and certain other industries whereas the Chinese government had spent from its own resources foreign exchange of $29.6 million.[3] The major contributions of ECA came sub-

3. *U.S. Economic Assistance to Formosa,* 1 January to 31 December 1950 (Washington, ECA, 1951), p. 45.

US AID PROGRAMS
(in thousands of dollars)

	Fiscal *year 1951–52*	Fiscal *year 1952–53*
Public health	250	160
Agriculture, forestry, fisheries	19,335	21,075
Transportation, power, etc.	5,630	4,550
Handicraft, manufacturing, mining and other industry	3,550	3,785
General engineering advisory services	650	690
Education	35	20
Public administration	255	345
Maintenance of essential supply ..	51,295	84,375
Total cost	81,000	115,000

sequently. During 1950 it allocated $11.7 million for various reconstruction activities, including $5.2 million for power, $3.9 million for railways, $1.5 million for highways, $0.3 million for telecommunications, and $0.76 million for other industries. Only $2.3 million of this, however, was for goods which had actually arrived by the end of the year.

Since the total of funds for Taiwan obligated by ECA during 1950 was about $33 million, it is evident that about one-third of the program budget was allocated for industrial maintenance and replacement. More than half of the program was in aid of agriculture, including the $17 million for fertilizer. Most of the rest of the program was for materials—such as raw cotton and crude oil used in local industry, or food substances such as wheat and soy beans. Even the latter, however, were further processed by mills in Formosa.

The distribution of US aid funds among different fields of activity in present and planned future programs is indicated in the above table.

The largest item in the program has become the maintenance of essential supply. This includes an item of $12.7 million for imports in support of military programs in 1951–52 and $35 million in 1952–53. The supply program accounts for 73.4 per cent of the total in the 1952–53 plan. Agriculture, forestry and fisheries come next in size, accounting for 18.3 per cent, with transportation, power and public works taking 4.0 per cent, handicrafts and manufacturing 3.3 per cent, and only one per cent for the rest of the program.[4]

4. *U.S. Technical and Economic Assistance in the Far East* (Washington, MSA, March 1952), p. 14.

CHAPTER EIGHT

Currency, Finance and Trade

A stable currency and balanced national finances are obviously essential if agricultural and industrial production on Formosa are to make headway. The runaway inflation on the mainland of China was certainly one of the important factors which undermined public confidence in the Nationalist Government and paved the way for the Communist victory. Similar inflationary conditions became manifest in Taiwan following the Chinese takeover. Then after the summer of 1948, when the catastrophe on the mainland led to the flooding of the island with refugees, uncontrolled inflation developed in Formosa also. In the summer of 1949, however, a currency reform was instituted which has been relatively effective, although inflationary pressures have continued to manifest themselves.

Inflation and Currency Reform

The Japanese yen in use on Formosa was exchanged at 15 to US$1 at the time of surrender. By the end of 1945 the rate had more than doubled. In May 1946 the provincial government introduced Chinese currency in place of the Japanese yen, but without changing the value; the new money was known as *taipi* (TP$), or Taiwan currency. By November 1946 the exchange rate was TP$150 to US$1, a jump of 1,000 per cent in little over a year. By the end of 1947 the *taipi* had depreciated another ten times, the rate being TP$1,500 to US$1.

In August 1948 the Nationalists carried out their abortive currency reform on the mainland, establishing the gold yuan (GY), which was expected to retain a stable value. The exchange rate of the *taipi* to the gold yuan was officially set at TP$1,835 to GY1. When the gold yuan, contrary to plan, inflated spectacularly, the *taipi* rate was not changed. As mainlanders simultaneously began to flood into Formosa, they were able to exchange their increasingly worthless gold yuan for Taiwan currency which would buy more. As a result local money and goods passed quickly into the hands of refugees at the expense of the resident population, while competitive bidding caused prices to skyrocket.

The government printing presses contributed to the process. At the time of the Japanese surrender 1.5 billion yen were in circulation. By the end of the year the number had been increased to 3 billion. During 1946 the amount of currency gradually expanded until by December the issue amounted to 5.3 billion with 6 billion as the announced ceiling. Nevertheless, during 1947 the presses continued their activity so that by the end of the year there were 15 billion *taipi* in circulation, and 20 billion by August 1948. But this was as nothing compared to the spurt in currency output which followed the inauguration of the gold yuan on the mainland. Within two months a new supply of TP$60 billion had been poured into the market and by the year's end currency reached the fantastic height of TP$180 billion. The exchange rate rose to TP$200,000 to US$1 by the beginning of 1949. Prices continued to rise at the rate of 30 per cent a month and more. Clearly the time had come for drastic action.

It was not until June 1949 that a new currency was introduced, the new *taipi* or NT$, at an announced rate of NT$5 to US$1. Old *taipi* were exchanged for the new bills at the rate of 40,000 to 1. Stringent measures were taken by the government, including full gold and foreign exchange backing for the new money, to keep its value stable, while efforts were made to balance the provincial and national budgets. Nevertheless, prices continued to rise, though at a more gradual and decelerating rate of increase. During the second half of 1949 the rate was about 14 per cent a month. By February 1950 prices leveled off and held relatively constant, even declining a bit, until August. During the fall of 1950 and early 1951 substantial price increases began to take place again.[1]

Meanwhile the exchange rate rose to NT$10 to US$1 by February 1950 and, with fluctuations, remained about 11.10 throughout the year, although 9.5 was quoted as the official rate. Toward the end of 1950 the exchange rate began to rise again, reaching 16 by March 1951.

The quantity of the new currency in circulation was limited by law to NT$200 million. An additional NT$50 million was authorized for subsidiary coinage and small notes and in July 1950 the issuance of another NT$50 million was authorized. The Bank of Taiwan was the sole legal issuing agency. Beginning with an issue of NT$31.9 million in June 1949, the new currency quickly rose to NT$111.6 million by September and then was augmented more gradually to NT$189 million by January 1950. The issue totaled NT$234 million in June 1950, when the new authority made possible an increase to NT$279 million in July. After this the volume of notes in circulation remained relatively constant until early 1951, when it began

1. See price indices given below, p. 116.

to rise again, reaching the total of NT$389 million in May, NT$473 million by the end of 1951 and NT$572 million by February 1952.[2]

With a total currency issue of less than the equivalent of US$30 million for a population of eight million people, or less than US$4 per person, it appeared to some that the issue was too small and there were complaints about the difficulty of obtaining money. Through the expansion of bank credit the government attempted to increase the amount of money available. Demand deposits in all banks rose from NT$72 million in June 1949 to NT$208.6 million by the beginning of 1950, NT$442.5 million by July, NT$713.6 million by May 1951 and about NT$1,400 million by February 1952.[3] Combining demand deposits and currency issued, the index of total money available increased from 100 in June 1949 to 944 by May 1951 and almost 1,700 by February 1952.

Bank of Taiwan loans were made available at the relatively low interest rate of 1.8 per cent per month. However, these funds went almost completely to public enterprises and government institutions, only a small amount going to private firms and individuals. Thus 40 per cent of the Bank of Taiwan's outstanding loans at the end of March 1951 were for military and governmental departments, chiefly of the provincial government. Productive enterprises obtained 30 per cent of the Bank's loans but these were largely government-owned concerns, only 5 per cent of total loans going to private companies. The remainder of the Bank's loans went to the distributive trade (19 per cent) and communications (5.6 per cent), almost all of which, again, was in government hands. Private concerns which could not obtain working capital from the

2. Bank of Taiwan, *Monthly Economic Review*, March 1952, p. 13.
3. *Ibid.*, July 15, 1951, p. 13, and March 1952, p. 13.

Bank of Taiwan (or from commercial banks, which lent at about 4 per cent per month) were forced to resort to the open market, where interest rates fluctuated but were generally in excess of 12 per cent per month.[4]

The most inflationary factor in the economy has been the huge budget of the National Government—especially its expenditures for military purposes—which has not been matched by current income. This was initially the case on the mainland, where the development of a runaway inflation caused disastrous repercussions on Taiwan. After the National Government moved to Taipei, this inflationary factor operated directly on the island's economy.

Provincial Government Finances

During the Japanese period the island's income more than paid for the costs of government, which amounted to only about half of Formosa's public revenue—the remainder being invested in the development of the economy. When the Chinese Nationalist authorities took over, they were naturally handicapped by the damage done during the war, by suspension of normal trade and loss of markets, and by the removal of Japanese administrative personnel. Nevertheless, they inherited all public properties and confiscated Japanese private property which has been roughly estimated as having the value of $2 billion. Moreover, they cancelled the island's public debt. They received from UNRRA during 1946 and early 1947 aid worth about $25 million and used for the island part of the aid rendered China by the United States. Yet by the end of 1946 the provincial government found that it had virtually no funds for education, public works or the tra-

---

4. *Ibid.*, May 15, 1951, pp. 4-5. By the end of 1951 the rate on loans dropped to around 10 per cent per month. *Ibid.*, March 1952, p. 8.

ditional subvention to county governments for the maintenance of local police. Provincial revenues meanwhile had declined from about $18 million in 1946 to the neighborhood of $5.5 million in 1947 and only $2 million in 1948. As the surplus taken from the Japanese was used up, the provincial authorities were unable to extract from declining current production enough income to maintain an adequate level of government operations.

By 1949, however, under the more vigorous administration of Chen Cheng and subsequently of K. C. Wu, tax reforms and increasing production made possible a larger provincial budget, equal to about $10.5 million in 1949. The 1950 budget increased spectacularly to about $30 million and the plan for 1951 called for income of about $35 million.[5]

The increase in provincial revenues was accomplished by a series of reforms in the system of taxation, relying chiefly on greater efficiency of collection and simplification with some reductions of the schedule, rather than on increased rates.[6]

5. These figures are derived from a table given by Han Lih-wu, *Taiwan Today* (Taipei, Hwa Kuo Publishing Co., 1951), p. 60, in terms of new *taipi*. He converted the figures for 1946–49 from old *taipi* to new *taipi* by dividing them by the exchange rate of 40,000 to 1. This gave him revenues in new *taipi* as follows: 1946, 70,209; 1947, 207,241; 1948, 1,574,508; 1949, 105,713,876; 1950, est. 319,968,297; 1951, est. 358,666,242. By converting the figures for the first three years back into their original form and then dividing by the exchange rates for each year, approximate equivalents in U.S. dollars were obtained. The 1949 figure was converted directly. Later data for 1950 and 1951 were obtained from Chinese News Service, Press Release, December 5, 1950, p. 4.

6. The difficulty of arriving at precise conclusions about the financial situation in Formosa is illustrated by discrepancies in reports about tax revenues given by two equally authoritative Chinese Nationalist sources: Han Lih-wu, *op. cit.*, p. 64, and

Even so, taxes have provided only about half of the provincial revenues, the rest coming largely from the government monopolies of cigarettes and wines, supplemented by sale of bonds and by lotteries. Income from the government monopolies has been a basic source of revenue for the provincial government. Estimates for 1950 anticipated NT$96 million but by October this figure had already been exceeded, according to Han. For 1951 Han states that NT$120 million should enter the island's coffers from the wine and cigarette monopoly, equalling one-third of the planned budget for the year. Figures on earlier years are unavailable.[7]

Chinese News Service, Press Release, February 6, 1951, p. 3. The national and provincial tax revenues collected in Formosa, in new *taipi,* are given for 1949 and 1950 as follows:

	1949		1950	
	Han Lih-wu	CNS	Han Lih-wu (Jan.-Oct.)	CNS
Income tax	3,869,899	5,546,995	29,597,908	37,953,217
Land tax	158,533,375	14,439,932	85,494,951	24,451,947
Inheritance tax ..	122,167	128,800	363,455	487,741
Stamp tax	3,309,118	3,547,517	11,214,135	33,996,452
Commodity tax ..	8,212,191	8,774,492	17,691,258	32,104,144
Mining tax	538,833	541,028	1,730,250	2,272,108
Business tax	7,847,765	7,541,591	19,717,041	21,489,896
Special business tax	304,826	997,233	5,365,651	3,785,967
Harbor construction tax	7,011,983	4,750,032	19,429,197	11,769,787
Fines	27,651	....	107,175	....
Land valuation tax	3,977,795	....	3,725,228	....
Educational reconstruction levy..	....	....	....	1,883,962
Total	193,755,603	46,267,621	194,436,349	170,195,222

Tax receipts during January and February 1951 amounted to NT$32.35 million, and estimates for the year come to about NT$240 million, according to the Bank of Taiwan (*Monthly Economic Review,* April 15, 1951, p. 1).

7. Han Lih-wu, *op. cit.,* p. 68.

With regard to the tax system, Han comments that "it is not as progressive as one might expect, for most taxes are indirect in nature and the tax rates are not so steep as to conform with the principle of equity." He adds that this is not unusual in "oriental countries" because of "practical difficulties in assessment of personal income and business profits." [8] This is certainly an understatement, since the monopoly income is virtually a vast sales tax, while the income tax constituted less than 3 per cent of provincial revenues in 1949, although it expanded to about 10 per cent in 1950. The land tax appears to have remained by all odds the most important source of tax revenue.

In addition to the monopolies it might be supposed that the government-operated industries would provide additional income for the public treasury. Yet neither Han nor any other authority on the subject gives figures on the net operations of the public enterprises. Presumably these large concerns are able to make substantial profits, but there is no indication that these profits contribute in any way to the provincial budget. Possibly a corporation tax might be levied on them. In 1946 a corporation capital tax yielded the equivalent of NT$34, according to Han, but this item dwindles to NT$1 in 1947 and thereafter disappears from the table of tax revenues. It is, of course, theoretically possible that all government enterprises broke exactly even each year, so that no record would appear on the government's books. It is notable that among the items of expenditure for Taiwan, reconstruction is given as the largest single item, accounting for 30 per cent of the planned budget for 1951. How this money is distributed, however, is not explained, although conceivably some of it may go to government corporations to restore

8. *Ibid.*, p. 61.

and enlarge basic equipment and facilities. It is recorded, however, that in 1950 the Taiwan Sugar Corporation, although owned by the Provincial Government, paid into the national treasury in profits and taxes the equivalent of about US$20 million.[9]

The third source of revenue for the provincial government is the sale of bonds and lottery tickets. In 1949 a bond issue of NT$90 million, at an interest rate of 4 per cent annually, repayable within fifteen years, was sold. Formosan separatists allege that the sale was accomplished by high-pressure means, and the fact that interest rates for ordinary loans were substantially higher (144 per cent for open market loans, even 21.6 per cent for Bank of Taiwan loans) would tend to confirm their view. A "patriotic saving lottery coupon" issue of NT$82.5 million was sold in 1950, repayable within five years. Beginning in April 1950 the government also sponsored a fortnightly lottery from which it had received, by the end of August, over NT$10 million, half of which was net profit after paying expenses and prizes.

As regards provincial expenditures after the 30 per cent for reconstruction, the budget for 1951 called for the use of 23.4 per cent for education and culture, 16 per cent for subsidies, 8.3 per cent for police and security, 8 per cent for economic development, 3.5 per cent for administrative costs (including 0.16 per cent for the provincial assembly), 3.6 per cent for health and medical costs, 2.09 per cent for social welfare and relief, and the rest for financial administration, trusteeships and a reserve fund.[10]

9. Chinese News Service, Press Release, June 5, 1951, p. 3. This information is attributed, not to Chinese sources, but to the report of an American engineering firm, presumably the J. G. White Corporation.
10. Han Lih-wu, *op. cit.*, p. 61.

The real difficulties of Formosan public finance stem, not from the costs of maintaining a provincial government and developing the island's economy, but from the heavy burden of supporting a national government including its military services. Precise information on the national budget does not seem to be available, although Han candidly remarks that the "National Government has not yet been able to balance its budget, even with the Provincial government sharing part of the defense expenditures since 1950." [11] Incidentally, his provincial budget figures for 1951 fail to show how much is allocated for the national budget. In April 1950 a Taipei spokesman declared that the provincial government, in addition to meeting its own expenses, contributed $410,000 monthly to the national budget.

National Government Budget

The central government also derives income from the salt monopoly (an estimated NT$60 million in 1950) and from customs receipts (NT$222.5 million in 1950, and NT$156.75 million in the first half of 1951). These revenues constituted only 60 per cent of required national expenditures, 86 per cent of which, according to Premier Chen Cheng on May 12, 1950, were spent for military purposes. Only 9.6 per cent of all national expenses went for support of the government's civilian agencies and another 4 per cent for service on the public debt.

It appears probable that the national government in 1950 was spending about US$11 million monthly, including $9.5 million for national defense. (If the armed forces contained 500,000 men, this would amount to $19 per man per month.) In order to remain solvent, Taipei sought a

11. *Ibid.*, p. 59.

subvention from the United States at the rate of $10 million monthly.[12]

On the basis of the $11 million monthly, the national budget in 1950 would have been over US$130 million. By December 31, 1950 ECA had authorized, since the beginning of its China operations, a total of $62.8 million out of appropriated funds. (An additional $3.6 million was financed by sale of commodities in Shanghai previously paid for by ECA.) Only $34 million in goods had actually arrived in Formosa. Moreover, some of this money was spent before 1950.

Under the military aid program Formosa was scheduled to receive about $75 million during the fiscal year 1950–51. It is doubtful if any of this was received during 1950, however.

Thus during 1950 US aid may have accounted for one-third of the national budget, through the income in local currency from the sale of ECA-financed imports.[13] In so far as the sales receipts of these goods, as in the case of fertilizer, may have exceeded the nominal exchange value of the ECA dollars, the actual aid to the national budget may have been greater than the dollar value of US aid would suggest.

All domestic revenues and foreign aid combined, however, still could not meet the spending requirements of the national budget. During the second half of 1949 national revenues accounted for only one-eighth of expenditures,

12. ECA, in a recent report, states that in 1950 "more than 70 per cent of total government expenditures were allocated for military purposes." This total included local, provincial and national budgets. *U.S. Economic Assistance to Formosa,* 1 January to 31 December 1950 (Washington, ECA, 1951), p. 5.

13. Burton Crane in the *New York Times,* January 3, 1951, stated that of ECA grants averaging $3.5 million a month, $1.9 million entered the national budget.

according to Finance Minister Yen Chia-kan. During 1950, however, they were reported to cover three-fourths of national spending, and an even larger proportion by 1951.[14] Additional income, therefore, had to be obtained through liquidation of capital assets and expansion of the note issue, especially through the authorization of an extra NT$50 million in July 1950 as noted above. The liquidation of assets included sale of government property (largely confiscated Japanese holdings) and foreign exchange, but especially of gold holdings. During 1949 the government had sold an average of 200,000 ounces of gold monthly. At approximately US$40 per ounce, that brought in $8 million a month or $96 million for the year, accounting for a very large share of the national budget. The government's gold reserve taken to Formosa by Chiang Kai-shek in the spring of 1949 has veen variously estimated at from $138 million to $300 million. Obviously it would be disastrous to the economy to continue to permit gold to be drained away at this rate, especially since a large metal reserve in the Bank of Taiwan was considered essential to bolster confidence in the currency. Yet in January 1950 the month's deficit was put at $8 million. In August 1950 Taipei asked Washington for a loan of $30 million to support its currency.

Meanwhile the government instituted a program of retrenchment, dismissing 150,000 persons in the armed forces, cutting down unnecessary administrative expenses and imposing strict controls on all use of funds. Increased attention was given to the collection of all possible taxes, including new heavy "defense surtaxes" and compulsory

14. Chinese News Service, Press Release, June 19, 1951, p. 2. According to ECA, however, revenues in 1950 covered only one-half of expenditures. *U.S. Economic Assistance to Formosa,* cited, p. 5.

purchase of "patriotic bonds." The support of measures to expand production was stressed. By September 1950 it was asserted that the monthly deficit had been cut to $1.4 million.

Nevertheless, by the end of 1950, dwindling gold and foreign exchange reserves made it clear that the national government, even with US aid, had not been living within its income. The only alternatives were: more American assistance, drastic curtailment of the military defense program, or a new bout of devastating inflation. Already the pressure on prices was making itself apparent. ECA in December 1950 authorized the shipment of $2.8 million in peanuts, textiles and other consumer goods as part of an emergency $5 million program intended to ward off inflation. In April 1951 the Taipei authorities again asked for an American loan of $30 million to stabilize the currency. Waning confidence in the Formosan dollar was indicated by a growing flight of capital. The exchange rate for American dollars had been NT$13.96 in January 1951 and had even declined to NT$13.13 in February. During March the evidence of deterioration appeared as the rate climbed to NT$16, while by the first week of April it had jumped to NT$18 per US$1.

On April 10, 1951 the Executive Yuan sought to counteract this trend by making all private dealings in gold and foreign currency illegal. Simultaneously a new system of foreign exchange certificates handled by the Bank of Taiwan was promulgated. The old preferential rate of NT$10.25 per US$1 was retained for use in paying for imports of essential commodities and for exports by government enterprises (e.g. sugar). The latter constitute over 80 per cent of all exports and government organs handle more than 30 per cent of all imports. A new exchange certificate system was set up, buying US dollars for NT$15.85, to apply to all other exporters and for importers who obtained approval for their purchases from the Production Finance Board. The exchange rates were liable to daily adjustment, presumably in accord with the relative purchasing power of the two currencies. However, in fact the rate of NT$15.85 was continued even though the ratio might have been higher if a free market had been permitted.[15]

A measure of the extent of the inflationary situation in Taiwan with which the Nationalist Government has been contending may be supplied by the index numbers for retail prices. By the end of 1950 the general index (Bank of Taiwan figures) stood at 275 as compared with a base of 100 for June 1949, representing a comparatively great achievement for the government in the face of tremendous inflationary pressures. By May 1951, however, the index had risen to 350.[16] By the end of 1951 it had gone to 480

15. Bank of Taiwan, *Monthly Economic Review,* May 15, 1951, pp. 1-3, 6. The black market rate was reported around NT$30 per U.S. dollar by the end of 1951. *New York Times,* January 3, 1952.

16. *Monthly Economic Review,* July 15, 1951, p. 4. Different indices used by the University of Taiwan showed a rise to 405 in December 1950 and 536 in May 1951, while the Provincial Government's Department of Finance released figures of 344 for December 1950 and 438 for May 1951. All used June 1949 as the base. However, the Bank of Taiwan's index employed a weighted geometric mean of the prices of twenty-four commodities, giving rice a very heavy weight; the University of Taiwan index was a simple geometric mean of the prices of eighteen commodities; and the Department of Finance used the latter method but included fifty commodities. Department of Finance figures are: July 1949, 108; January 1950, 218; July 1950, 246; December 1950, 344; May 1951, 438. During 1950 the currency depreciated about 80 per cent and during the first ten months of 1951 another 40 per cent, according to the *New York Times,* January 2, 1951, based on Department of Finance figures.

and at the end of February 1952 it stood at 527.[17] It was apparent that Taipei still faced formidable difficulties in attempting to stabilize the financial situation.

Preliminary estimates showed the total national and local government expenditures during 1951 as equal to more than NT$2 billion. At the black market rate of NT$30, this would amount to less than US$70 million, and even at the foreign trade certificate rate of NT$15.60, to less than US$130 million. Even so, with US aid payments during the year valued at US$68 million the deficit at the year's end was estimated at NT$150 to NT$200 million (on the order of US$10 million).[18]

To help meet the inflationary situation in Formosa the ECA not only contributed funds but sought actively to assist in the control of the economy. It cooperated with the Taipei authorities in setting up and operating an Economic Stabilization Board, and began to develop programs intended to strengthen public administration as a means both of increasing governmental efficiency and of reducing costs.

Formosa's Foreign Trade

Taiwan's monetary difficulties were intimately related to its negative trade balance. It is appropriate at this point, therefore, to turn to an analysis of the Formosan trade pattern.

Ever since the Dutch and Spanish manifested an interest in Formosa, the island has played an important role in Far Eastern commerce. Sitting astride the major North-South sea lanes off the East Asian coast, it has provided

17. *Monthly Economic Review,* March 1952, p. 12. This is a general index of commodity wholesale prices compiled by the daily *Economic Times.*
18. *Ibid.,* July 15, 1951, p. 4.

harbors for transshipment and hide-outs for pirates. Under Japanese rule, the products of Formosan agriculture and the local market assumed a growing commercial significance.

This Japanese-sponsored trade consisted chiefly of the export of sugar and rice in exchange for numerous manufactured goods. Fortunately for the people of the island, output of food more than kept pace with a growing population. In order to maintain a high level of agricultural production, however, the island came to depend on substantial imports of fertilizer from Japan. Thus the disruption of normal trade which characterized the first post-war years not only deprived the Taiwanese of manufactured items to whose consumption they had become accustomed but also made it impossible to maintain pre-war standards of food production.

Although exports went from Formosa to Shanghai and elsewhere in substantial volume after VJ-Day, the proceeds from these sales were generally not available for the purchase of needed imports since they were appropriated by persons intending to use the money in China. With the Communist conquest of the mainland, however, the Nationalist leaders found that their island position necessitated the stimulation of an expanding and balanced commerce. To establish a firm economic foundation, Formosa will have to increase the domestic manufacture, where practicable, of items otherwise imported, such as fertilizers and textiles, and at the same time stimulate the production of export crops or products which can reduce the present undue dependence on the sale of costly sugar.

The nature of the traditional trade pattern may be seen more specifically by examining pre-war statistics. The following table shows the value in US dollars and per cent of total trade of certain important items:

FORMOSAN EXPORTS, 1939

	U.S. $ (millions)	Per cent
Sugar	67.5	43.8
Rice	33.4	21.7
Bananas	4.4	2.9
Canned pineapple	3.5	2.3
Tea—Oolong and Pouchong	3.4	2.2
Camphor	1.6	1.0
Timber	1.3	0.9
All others	39.0	25.3
Total	153.9	100.0

FORMOSAN IMPORTS, 1939

	U.S. $ (millions)	Per cent
Sulphate of ammonia	5.5	5.2
Cotton and silk cloth	5.1	4.8
Bean cake	5.3	5.0
Fish, dried and salted	2.5	2.4
Gunny bags	2.4	2.3
Paper	1.9	1.8
Cigarettes	1.4	1.3
Sake	1.8	1.7
All others	80.0	75.4
Total	106.1	100.0

In 1939, 89.5 per cent of Taiwan's exports went to Japan and 9 per cent to Korea and Manchuria, under Japanese control. Only 5.7 per cent of total exports went to China and 1.6 per cent to the United States, with very small amounts going to other countries. A similar situation existed with regard to imports, Japan providing 83.4 per cent and Korea and Manchuria 12 per cent. Only 1.0 per cent of imports came from China and 0.4 per cent from the United States. Some, but probably a small percentage, of the trade with Japan consisted of goods originating from or ultimately destined for other countries, but trans-shipped through Japan.

Foreign trade statistics for the post-war period are notably fragmentary, especially for the first few years. By 1949, when it had become clear to Nationalist leaders that their future would depend on the strength of their position in Taiwan, the foreign trade deficit was equal to about $34 million: the difference between imports worth $100 million and exports that earned $66 million. Of the imports, $14 million were for munitions and other defense equipment paid for by the United States. Thus the actual deficit in the balance of payments to be paid for by the sale of gold and foreign exchange amounted to about $20 million.

During 1950 the trade deficit grew and there was some increase in the value of total transactions. All visible imports were valued at $119 million, while exports were worth $72 million, leaving a negative balance of $46.9 million. Since reparations from Japan paid for about $7 million, the actual deficit was almost $40 million. Of this amount, ECA paid for $20.5 million, leaving a little more than $19 million to be financed by the Nationalists out of their gold and foreign exchange reserves.

Comparable figures regarding the trade situation in 1951 are not yet available. Taiwan customs statistics for May and June, however, show that of total imports during those months about 60 per cent belonged in a category made up largely of ECA-financed goods. It seems probable that a progressively larger part of the economy's imports is being financed through American grants, which amounted to $68 million in paid shipments during 1951. Bank of Taiwan figures based on foreign exchange transactions show a favorable balance, but this may be accounted for by failure to include figures on US imports.

It is apparent that without the support of ECA funds, the economic position of Formosa would soon become disastrous. The dangers which confront the island are made more apparent when one recalls the extreme dependence on sugar exports as a source of foreign exchange. With the output for sugar in 1950 estimated at little more than half that of 1949 (340,000 tons as compared with 612,000 tons) Taiwan faced a great drop in exports. Even so, sugar remains the main export item, accounting, for example, for $7.85 million out of a total of $9.62 million exported in February 1952.[19]

The government's strict exchange control system has provided a means for restricting imports to essential items. Nevertheless, and even with the benefit of ECA aid, Taipei has had to eat heavily into its assets in order to balance its overseas accounts.

Balance of Payments

In order to complete the picture of the economy's international position, it is necessary to take into account not only the balance on account of visible transactions, but also various invisible imports and exports. As noted above, the difference between expenditures for imports and earnings from exports during 1950 was equivalent to $46.9 million. Invisible items, such as payments on loans, foreign travel, receipts and expenditures for diplomatic and consular establishments and international conferences and organizations, and the like, resulted in a net loss of $5 million. Moreover, Taipei imported $2.5 million worth of gold more than it exported during the year. (Imports were $4.3 million and exports $1.8 million.) When these sums are added together, it may be seen that Formosa had to finance a total negative balance of $54.45 million.

19. *Ibid.,* March 1952, p. 14.

To pay for this the Formosan economy benefited from donations worth $31.7 million, made up largely of ECA funds, but including also reparations and remittances from overseas Chinese. The difference, then, was $22.7 million, which had to be found by drawing on the assets of the economy or by borrowing. This amount was made up by selling foreign deposits in the amount of $12 million and incurring new liabilities to the extent of $8 million. The discrepancy is accounted for in the Chinese figures under the heading of "errors and omissions."

These figures do not give an adequate picture of the National Government's balance of payments, however, for they do not include the domestic sales of monetary gold. During the year the Bank of Taiwan, as agent for the National Government, sold 1.4 million ounces of gold more than it bought. At $35 per ounce, this brought in $48.2 million. Except for the gold which may have been smuggled out of the country, this amount remained as part of the total capital of the people of the island. Nevertheless, from the government's point of view, it must be counted as a negative item in its balance of current transactions. It was balanced by an equal item in the column for net movement of capital and monetary gold, representing a decline in total assets. If this item is included in the picture, the conclusion may be reached that the total negative balance on current transactions was $71 million ($48.2 plus $22.7). This was paid for by a net reduction of total assets equal to $67 million. The difference of almost $4 million in the sums is attributed to errors in calculations and estimates.[20]

20. This analysis is based on the figures submitted by the Chinese government to the Bank for International Settlements, as given in the Bank of Taiwan's *Monthly Economic Review* for June 15, 1951, p. 1. These data as given in outline are as follows (in millions of U.S. dollars):

Figures for the balance of payments in 1951 are not yet available. Nevertheless, it is clear from the foregoing analysis that in order to maintain its position at home and abroad the National Government in Formosa has had to

A. CURRENT TRANSACTIONS	Credit	Debit	Balance
1. Merchandise			
1.1 Export and import	72.43	91.59	—19.16
1.2 Reparations		7.27	— 7.27
1.3 ECA imports		20.48	—20.48
2. Non-monetary gold		50.77	—50.77
(Includes: foreign transactions, —2.54; monetary gold decrease, —48.23)			
3. Investment income		1.03	— 1.03
4. Travel		0.12	— 0.12
5. Government, not included elsewhere			
5.1 Diplomatic and consular..	0.30	3.00	— 2.70
5.2 International conferences..		0.13	— 0.13
5.3 Contribution to international organizations		0.32	— 0.32
6. Miscellaneous			
6.1 Film rentals		0.30	— 0.30
6.2 Communications		0.06	— 0.06
6.3 Clean bills bought	6.36		+ 6.36
6.4 Outward remittances		6.70	— 6.70
7. Donations			
7.1 Overseas remittances	3.96		+ 3.96
7.2 Reparations	7.27		+ 7.27
7.3 ECA	20.48		+20.48
8. Total current transactions	110.80	181.77	—70.97
Errors and omissions			3.86

B. MOVEMENT OF CAPITAL AND MONETARY GOLD
(Increases or decreases in each column indicated by + or —)

	Assets	Liabilities	Net assets
9. Long-term capital			
9.1 Amortization		—1.00	+ 1.00
10. Short-term capital			
10.1 Payments and clearing agreements		+7.79	— 7.79
10.2 Foreign currencies	+ 4.86		+ 4.86
10.3 Foreign deposits	—16.95		—16.95
11. Monetary gold	—48.23		—48.23
12. Total movement of capital and monetary gold	—60.32	+6.79	—67.11

draw very heavily on its gold reserves and at the same time to rely upon substantial subventions from the United States ($68 million in paid shipments during 1951).

Dependence on US Aid

It is clear that the Formosan economy, because of its heavy military expenditures and excess of imports over exports, has suffered from both a large budgetary deficit at home and a foreign exchange gap internationally. ECA and its successor, MSA, have closed both these gaps through the financing of imports. Thus the 1951–52 MSA program is paying for about $80 million worth of supplies and equipment. During the calendar year 1952 foreign exchange payments are expected to equal about $200 million, whereas foreign exchange earnings may amount to only about $120 million—the gap of $80 million to be closed by American aid.

At the same time Formosan internal government costs—local, provincial and national—will exceed $300 million during 1952, according to MSA estimates, of which half (or 80 per cent of the national budget) will be military costs. Total revenues, however, may be in the neighborhood of $230 million. The budget gap of roughly $70 million will be largely closed through the use of domestic counterpart funds obtained through the sale of MSA-financed commodity imports. Part of the national government expenditures will, of course, be incurred because of the US-supported military program. These local costs will also be paid out of the counterpart funds. The direct military assistance program for 1951–52—about $200 million —may also help with these costs.

While the MSA program helps to balance the governmental budget, it will simultaneously serve to counteract inflationary pressures, since the sale of American-financed imports will provide more commodities with which to meet the demand created by increases in governmental expenditures. The US aid program, therefore, is making possible the stabilization of the entire Formosan economy. Correspondingly the continued balance of the Nationalist Government depends on a continuation of that aid.

By way of recapitulation it may be convenient at this point to summarize the general trend of US assistance. Up to June 1950 in several earlier programs a total of less than $28 million had been actually spent in Formosa. After the outbreak of the Korean war, and under the new Mutual Security program, the allotment for Taiwan increased to a total of $143 million for the period from June 1950 to the end of 1951. Of this allotment, however, only $71 million had been paid out for actual shipments by December 31, 1951. Including previous programs, the grand total spent in Taiwan by the end of 1951 was therefore in the neighborhood of $100 million. (These figures do not include direct military aid.)

In terms of fiscal year appropriations, the amounts for 1950–51 and 1951–52 were $98 million and $81 million respectively. For 1952–53 the amount sought by the Mutual Security Agency was $115 million.

The following statement taken from a recent MSA report indicates the chief accomplishments of the program: [21]

—Major support to military forces—through common-use items; reconstruction and expansion of transportation, electric power and other essential facilities; allocation of counterpart funds to military construction, etc.—

—Price instability and budget deficits substantially reduced—1950 rate of increase in wholesale prices

21. *U.S. Technical and Economic Assistance in the Far East* (Washington, MSA, March 1952), p. 15.

halved during 1951; 1951 ordinary revenues up 60
percent over 1950, with further increase budgeted
for 1952; more effective expenditure controls adopted
with MSA and MAAG guidance—

—Output of foods basic to local consumption above pre-
war (Japanese regime) peaks—sweet potatoes up 20
percent, wheat 165 percent, and peanuts 89 percent—

—Rice production, aided by U.S.-financed fertilizer, at
record level in 1951; substantial quantities exported—

—JCRR highly successful in striking at basic causes of
agrarian unrest through work in fields such as land
tenure, rural health, seed improvement, rural education, supervision of fertilizer distribution, pest control, etc.—

—Fewer Communists, less unrest, more security of person
in Formosa than any other country in Far East—

—Industrial and mining production materially expanded
—coal production now 1,450,000 tons as compared with
776,000 in 1945; cement, 389,000 tons as compared
with 193,000 in 1947; flour milled now 380,000 tons
as compared with 67,000 in 1946—

—Electric power capacity at all-time high (217,000 KW)—

—Railroad carloadings approximately tripled since 1946
and 50 percent above 1948—

—Fertilizer production more than three times prewar—

—Textile output tripled since 1950; self-sufficiency near
in cotton cloth production (result of MSA-financed
raw cotton from U.S. plus increased spindleage)—

—Surpluses for export reached or in prospect for coal,
aluminum, cement—

—Calendar 1952 exports conservatively estimated at U.S.
$110 to $115 million, against U.S. $90 million in
1951—

—Steel spans fabricated for 6500-foot highway bridge (at
Silo) linking northern and southern highway systems, and scheduled for erection in 1952—

—Self-help determination rising—

—Morale greatly improved—

—Relations between Formosan and mainland Chinese improved—

—Free enterprise strongly fostered through supplying of raw materials to private industries, increased use of private commercial channels in procuring MSA supplies, and encouragement to sale of government-owned enterprises to private ownership—

The signature of a peace treaty on April 28, 1952 between the Nationalist Government and Japan may lead to further development of trade relations between the two countries. So long as Formosa is not integrated economically with the mainland, it can be sustained only by heavy US subventions, or great expansion of its trade with Japan, or both.

PART FOUR

SOCIAL

CHAPTER NINE

Public Health, Education and Labor

The economic, political and military aspects of the Formosan situation are not the only ones which need to be
considered in framing American policy. Attention should
also be given to the record of the Nationalist Government
in dealing with various social questions because of their
direct impact on the attitude of the people toward their
government and their effect on the nation's productive and
military capacities. For reasons of space only three typical
social questions have been singled out for analysis here:
public health, education and labor.

Public Health under the Japanese

Developments in the field of public health have exhib-
ited features typical of those in many other spheres of post-
war Formosan life.

Under the Japanese, the imperial rulers, with characteristic industriousness, and primarily from a concern for social stability and economic progress, had instituted a comprehensive public health system immediately upon their
assumption of responsibility for the island's administration. The effectiveness of their program may be judged
from the fact that annual deaths per thousand were reduced from 34 in 1906 to 20.5 by 1935.

Among the more notorious afflictions on the island when the Japanese came were recurrent epidemics of bubonic plague and cholera. By 1911 the former had been virtually eliminated and the latter was brought under control by 1920. In dealing with plague comprehensive port quarantine procedures were inaugurated: all ships arriving from plague-infested areas were inspected and subjected to rat-extermination measures as well as other precautions. The campaign against cholera was part of the more general struggle against unsanitary conditions which facilitated the transmission of enteric diseases. Systems of sewage and refuse disposal were established. Strict regulations governing the handling and distribution of food were enforced. Campaigns against the house fly were carried out. As a result of virtually universal vaccination, smallpox was wiped out.

Equally important was the battle against malaria, not only a major killer but also a widespread debilitating disease. It caused 13,350 deaths in 1915 but only 3,782 in 1935, and by 1940 it had been practically eliminated in the vicinity of Taipei, although occasional cases occurred elsewhere. These results were accomplished by a program of public education on malaria prevention measures, and the cleaning up of mosquito breeding spots. Over half of the population was examined and given blood tests, the malaria bearers being given appropriate treatment.

To supplement sanitary and public health measures, the Japanese stimulated the development of hospitals and medical facilities. By 1940 there were 249 hospitals, of which 33 were public and government institutions and the remainder under private operation. The latter were small clinics with capacities ranging from ten to fifty beds, but several of the government hospitals had substantial facilities. About 6,000 beds were available on the island. Whereas less than 64,000 patients received hospital treatment in

1897, more than 726,000 obtained such service in 1907 and by 1938 over a million persons received hospital care. In addition to general hospitals there were special institutions for tuberculosis, leprosy and mental diseases and venereal disease, as well as opium research laboratories. A central research institute serviced the government hospitals. The University Medical School trained doctors and gave special attention to the study of tropical diseases.

As regards personnel, there were over 2,000 "doctors," although a relatively small number of these, largely Japanese, were fully qualified physicians. Most of the rest were native Formosans who were given a "special course" which qualified them for limited medical and public health practice in rural areas and smaller towns, where they often received government subsidies to help them make their contribution to the development of the general health program. More than 1,500 women were also trained as midwives in an effort to reduce infant mortality rates. Though behind contemporary Western practice, the medical and public health facilities of Formosa were in advance of anything realized on the south and east Asian mainland.

Post-war Health Measures

The end of the war necessarily brought serious disruption. The withdrawal of Japanese personnel was a serious blow, although many Formosan partially trained doctors remained. Physical facilities had suffered much bomb damage and the rubble of war-devastated areas provided new breeding grounds for the malarial mosquito. Moreover, the Japanese had failed to teach most of the Formosans the reasons for many of their public health measures, which had been sternly enforced by the police on the basis of conformity with official regulations. Consequently the populace took advantage of the new situation to revert to many traditional unhygienic practices.

But the people of Taiwan had become accustomed to the advantages of a public health program, even if they did not understand its details. Among their leaders, moreover, were men who thoroughly comprehended the reasons for sanitary precautions. They took the lead, therefore, in protesting against the policies of the new Chinese administration in this field.

The direction of the public health administration was entrusted to a pharmacologist without previous experience in this kind of work. Whether justifiably or not, the opinion became widespread that he was more concerned with the management of extensive drug interests than with the promotion of public health. At the same time mercenary considerations now appeared to control every facet of public health activity: granting of licenses, provision of services and materials, sale of confiscated Japanese equipment and drugs. Even UNRRA found its relief and medical activities hampered when they appeared to trespass on spheres where the new authorities had established special interests. Established services, such as examination of school children, vaccinations, anti-malaria precautions, etc., lapsed and subsidies were no longer provided for rural practitioners who could not support themselves in poor districts on a private fee basis.

Deterioration of public health services manifested itself in a recurrence of long extinct epidemic diseases. In the spring of 1946 cholera reappeared and began to spread rapidly in the southwestern districts. Between April 1 and November 1, 2,691 cases were recorded, of which 1,460 were fatal. To meet the emergency UNRRA doctors and nurses with the aid of UNRRA personnel moved in and, despite official resistance, took over control of the situation. Local government administrators and doctors at first refused to treat cases after office hours and restricted the release of medical supplies to the normal amounts. By dint of great exertions, however, the outside personnel together with native Formosan assistants and some Chinese mainland doctors and nurses were finally able to bring the epidemic under control.

Similarly smallpox became epidemic after 1946 with 6,000 cases reported by August 1947. The disruption of the quarantine service in the ports, due to several politically motivated changes of the administrative system, had made possible the reintroduction of the disease by new arrivals from the mainland. For the same reason bubonic plague once again broke out in 1947. Prompt quarantine measures instituted by UNRRA personnel brought a quick halt to plague, but smallpox was not wiped out until mid-1950.

Despite these serious setbacks, important progress has been registered in the last couple of years. UNRRA, while it was in operation, and subsequently the World Health Organization, have rendered signal aid and helped to overcome bureaucratic obstacles to the reestablishment of an effective public health system. Since ECA has begun to operate in Taiwan, JCRR has made rural health work one of its major emphases. It assisted, for example, in the rehabilitation of seventy-seven rural water supply plants which had fallen into disrepair, bringing benefits to about 200,000 persons in rural areas. JCRR has also supported training programs for rural public health nurses and midwives and strengthened rural health centers. In the long-term anti-malaria campaign, JCRR has assisted the malaria research institute, established by the Rockefeller Foundation in 1946, when the withdrawal of Foundation support in 1949 threatened to terminate this useful work. It has also subsidized 70 of the 128 malaria prevention stations which have been reestablished—compared with 200 in the Japanese period.

With the reinvigoration of the Taipei government, the public health bureau has been expanded into an independent department under the provincial government. With JCRR support, especially in the provision of medical supplies, 270 village and town health stations had been established by 1950, with plans for the setting up of 120 more.

In connection with garbage and sewage disposal, which was one of the worst casualties of the Chen Yi administration, Dr. Han comments that "compared with the period of Japanese rule, certain sanitary conditions . . . may not be as good." [1] But he goes on to state that because of the work of the health stations and improved medicines, the island's death rate had decreased from 17.5 per thousand in 1942 to 12.62 in 1949, although he concedes that some allowance ought to be made for unreported cases. Infant mortality rates, he says, have likewise fallen from 155.36 per thousand in 1934 to 77.5 in 1948 and 47.86 in 1949. It would seem, therefore, that following the vicissitudes of the first post-war years, the Chinese administration on Taiwan, with considerable foreign assistance, has been able to reestablish public health conditions which do not compare too unfavorably with those achieved under the Japanese, and no doubt excel in good measure conditions on the Chinese mainland.

Japanese Educational Policy

The traditional respect of the Chinese for education is reflected in the final sentence of Han Lih-wu's monograph on Taiwan, which reads: "It is the National Government's determination to plan and realize an education that is free,

1. Han Lih-wu, *Taiwan Today* (Taipei, Hwa Kuo Publishing Co., 1951), p. 52.

equal and rational, an education that will contribute to human welfare, social happiness, political democracy and economic prosperity in Taiwan." [2]

The Nationalist leaders possessed an excellent opportunity to work toward these goals by reason of the rather highly developed educational facilities bequeathed to them by the Japanese. More than 1,000 primary schools (six-year course) widely scattered over the island provided facilities for 850,000 pupils, or more than 70 per cent of the school age (6 to 12) population. Since attendance by girls was considerably lower than by boys, male school attendance must have been almost universal. Opportunities for secondary education were more limited, about 40,000 Formosans being enrolled in 165 institutions. The university and colleges for higher education had a total enrollment of less than 1,800, and of this number only about 350 were Formosans, the remainder being Japanese.

In general, the policy of Japan had been to provide elementary education and technical and vocational training on an upper primary level for the native population and to restrict opportunities for advanced training chiefly to the Japanese residents. Nevertheless, some Formosans were able to enter the colleges and the university and some 75,000 islanders in all, according to a rough estimate, went to Japan for middle and higher educational training. Moreover, certain types of profession, such as rural medicine, were open to Taiwanese, and received encouragement from the Japanese. The aim of Japanese policy was to create a docile but competent subject people whose obedient industry would contribute to the economic welfare of the empire. The byproduct of Japanese policy, however, was a literate population, exceptionally well educated by comparison with mainland Chinese standards. It included many

2. *Ibid.*, p. 157.

persons competent in the operation of modern mechanical and technical devices and a fair quota of trained leaders.

Chinese Educational Policy

The initial impact of the Chen Yi administration upon the island's educational system was devastating. Funds were largely cut off and Japanese administrators and teachers were replaced by incompetent hangers-on of the ruling clique. The language problem also provided a major difficulty. Under the Japanese, primary schools for the Formosans had been conducted in the local dialect but secondary and higher education were exclusively in Japanese, while even primary pupils were required to learn to read in Japanese. The Nationalists immediately abolished the use of Japanese and made Mandarin, the official national language, compulsory in the schools. But appropriate textbooks were not available and students as well as local teachers were generally unable to use the new medium.

Resulting discontent within the school system began to assume an open and violent aspect. Middle school students especially took the lead in political agitation against the Nationalist regime. As on the mainland, student movements were extremely influential in molding public opinion. When popular disaffection reached its peak in the incidents of March 1947, the students were selected by the Chen Yi administration as one of the chief targets for violent suppression, many being massacred during the ensuing period of terrorism.

In the course of time, however, conditions began to improve. New textbooks were prepared and distributed. As the flood of refugees poured into Formosa more competent mainlanders were found to fill administrative and teaching posts and the position of native staff members also appears to have improved somewhat. Increased funds were put into the school system as the appropriation for education rose from 8.4 per cent of the provincial budget in 1946 to about 25 per cent in 1950. The proportion of school age children in school also increased gradually to almost 80 per cent by 1950. According to a five-year program announced by the government, 95 per cent of the children would be in school by 1955.

Enrollment in primary schools showed a slight increase following the declines of the first post-war years. By 1950 there were 892,000 pupils registered in almost 1,200 schools. In 1949 there had been 17,000 teachers in these schools, of whom one-third were found by the administration to be "unqualified." To remedy this situation the authorities announced that the unqualified personnel would have to take further training or be replaced.

There appears to have been a more substantial increase in secondary school enrollment. In 1947 there were about 60,000 secondary, normal and vocational school students but by 1950 the number had risen to almost 115,000. In large part, however, this increase may be explained by the influx of relatively well-off mainlanders whose children entered the middle schools. Figures showing the number of Formosans registered in these institutions are not available. Another factor contributing to this increase was the reduction of special technical and vocational institutions at the secondary and upper primary level which had been developed by the Japanese. These were largely abolished by the Chinese in order to establish the uniform system of primary and secondary schools, patterned in large part on the American model, in vogue on the mainland. Presumably many of the students who would have entered these vocational schools entered the secondary institutions instead. The Chinese planned to introduce vocational and technical courses in the middle schools in order to achieve the ends previously attained by the special Japanese schools. The number of secondary schools recorded a sharp increase in 1947.[3] The increase may in part be explained by the subdivision of six-year secondary institutions into two three-year institutions: junior and senior middle schools. In 1950 there were 206 secondary schools, according to Han, utilizing the services of about 7,000 teachers. Of these about 2,000 were considered unqualified and subject to retraining or replacement.

With regard to higher education, the chief institution under the Japanese was the Taiwan Imperial University, which operated faculties of literature and political science, of science and agriculture, and of medicine, as well as research institutes of tropical agriculture and tropical medicine. In addition there were three technical colleges giving training in economics, agriculture and forestry, and engineering. Under the Nationalist regime, the university was renamed the National Taiwan University. The technical college of economics was transferred to the university, where it became part of a new faculty of law. The technical colleges of agriculture and engineering—offering two to three-year courses—were expanded to four-year colleges, and a technical college of local administration was opened in Taipei in 1949. A Normal College was also opened in Taipei.

In 1945 enrollment in higher educational institutions was about 1,700. It subsequently declined and remained at around 1,300 until 1948. The following year, however, the figure jumped to almost 6,000, including, according to

3. According to Han Lih-wu, *ibid.*, p. 150, the number was 165 in 1945, 221 in 1946 and 215 in 1947. However, Education Commissioner Fan Shou-kang, in January 1947, gave the figures of 174 middle schools in 1944, 70 in 1945 and 208 in 1947. *Chunghua Jih Pao*, January 31, 1947, cited in Joshua Liao manuscript.

Han, about 3,500 native Formosans and 2,400 mainlanders. Han notes that because the standards of mainland students in Chinese and English were, on the whole, higher than those of Formosans, there was danger that higher educational opportunities for indigenous pupils might be restricted. Consequently local students were marked on a preferential basis in the entrance examinations and a quota of 70 per cent for Taiwanese was fixed in the colleges. In 1950 Han states that the quota system was abolished but it had become unnecessary since "local students did as well or even better than refugee students." Joshua Liao, a Formosan separatist, takes a less rosy view of the situation, declaring that in the autumn of 1948 80 per cent of the applicants who passed the entrance examination of the university were mainlanders who had done much better on decisive questions relating to Chinese history and literature. If Han's figures are correct, we may assume that measures were subsequently taken to bring about a more equitable distribution of available facilities between Formosans and mainland Chinese.

It seems unlikely that all the complaints of the Formosan separatist leaders have been satisfied and undoubtedly a large percentage of available resources for secondary and higher instruction, as well as teaching posts, have been utilized by mainlanders—thus perpetuating a situation somewhat similar to that which prevailed under the Japanese, a situation which undoubtedly aroused much ire among Formosan leaders. Nevertheless, it seems apparent that in the last year or two real progress has been made, not only in the raising of educational standards and the expansion of the school system, but also in the provision of more resources for utilization by the Taiwanese themselves.

Industrial Labor

A third area in which the policies of the government have important social effects is that of labor, especially questions affecting the employment conditions of industrial workers. Before the war it was estimated that 70 per cent of all gainfully occupied men were employed in agriculture. Figures of 15 per cent for industry and transportation and 10 per cent for trade have also been given. At best such estimates are but rough approximations because of the high degree of mobility between agricultural and industrial pursuits. Most workers maintained close contact with their original farm homes, to which they could readily go whenever they were without employment.

The relatively small size of the island and the excellent transportation facilities made this mobility possible. The fact that a large part of the island's industry consisted of the secondary processing of agricultural crops, and that much of the work thereby created was seasonal in character, also confirmed the close intertwining of agricultural and industrial pursuits. Moreover, the relatively high income of the farm population and the absence of famines meant that there was no group of impoverished rural folk forced to seek their livelihood in the urban areas. Workers often lived in their farm homes and commuted to nearby factories and installations. Others, especially small shopkeepers and tradesmen, frequently maintained their families in country establishments while they carried on their vocations in city shops.

In 1936, according to Japanese figures, there were over 81,000 industrial workers in shops employing more than six workers. Since a very large part of industry consisted of small domestic establishments, especially in the processing of food, such as rice polishing, it is likely that the total number of wage-earners was in the neighborhood of 200,000.

During the late thirties and the war years, the Japanese stepped up the island's industrial activities, especially in relation to military production. Moreover, the conscription of Formosans for labor service overseas cut heavily into the available supply of manpower. The result was a shortage of workers and competitive bidding among rival concerns which tended to improve wages and working conditions, while unemployment was unknown.

Following the take-over the situation underwent a drastic change. The influx of mainlanders who occupied both administrative and manual labor positions in the chief urban centers caused unemployment among Formosans and a flow of labor back to rural homesteads. The difficulties of the situation were aggravated by the return of more than 50,000 Formosans from overseas, most of whom were impoverished conscript workers left stranded by the Japanese on the island of Hainan at the war's end. But the underlying cause of the serious dislocation was simply the collapse of production which resulted partly from wartime damage and deterioration of equipment, but chiefly from the carpetbagging policies of the Chen Yi administration. According to estimates by UNRRA personnel, employment in manufacturing industries, which had been between 40,000 and 50,000 before the war, had fallen to 5,000 by fourteen months after VJ-Day.

With the subsequent revival of industrial production, employment simultaneously increased. By December 1949 there were 67,660 persons working in private industry, and 79,058 in public industry by September 1950, a total of 156,718, according to figures cited by Han Lih-wu.[4] Dr. Han's figures, however, do not give any indication

4. Han Lih-wu, *op. cit.,* p. 122.

of how many of these were native Formosans and how many were refugees from the mainland. The figure of 1.5 million is often given as an approximate estimate of the number of Chinese immigrants from the mainland, but no breakdown is available to show how many of these were adult males. Presumably most of the 500,000 members of the armed forces were without their families. It would be unlikely if men of working age constituted less than one-fifth of the remainder so it may be assumed that there were more than 200,000 potential workers from the mainland. Of these about 30,000 were employed by the provincial government. The rest must be employed by the national government or in industrial and commercial occupations —since very few, if any, have been able to take up farming—or else are unemployed. There can be no doubt that unemployment among both Formosans and mainland refugees is substantial but conflicting estimates of the scale of unemployment appear to be very unreliable.

Chinese Labor Policy

As a means of stabilizing employment conditions and reducing labor unrest, the government in March 1950 announced the promulgation of a system of labor insurance. Long-term and seasonal employees in both public and private enterprise were to receive accident, disability, birth, death and old age coverage. It was hoped that ultimately sickness and unemployment benefits would be added. Premiums at the rate of 3 per cent of the worker's monthly wage were to be paid, 60 per cent by the employee, 20 per cent by the employer and 20 per cent by the provincial government. By the end of June 1951 it was announced that 140,651 laborers were covered by the system. According to Dr. Han 200,000 employed workers would be eligible,[5] but a dispatch from Taipei published in the *New York Times* on January 3, 1951 gave 280,000 as the total employed manual laborers. By January 1951 benefits totaling almost NT$3.4 million had been paid out to almost 11,000 cases, or an average of a little over NT$300 each—roughly about $30.

It is notable that the chief agitation among the Formosans against the Nationalist regime and for improvement of their lot has come from local leaders in the professions and commerce, and from students and intellectuals. Many of these, moreover, have derived from relatively well-to-do Formosan landowners who could afford to provide a costly education for their children. The lack of conspicuous agitation among peasant and labor groups, however, cannot be taken as proof that these elements of the population have been fully satisfied.

In the twenties, largely under the leadership of Japanese trade unionists, a Taiwan peasants' union was formed—chiefly among sugar plantation workers—which by 1926 claimed 24,000 members. Simultaneously the workers in various crafts—metallurgical, building, masonry, mechanical workers, etc.—organized about thirty trade unions which united in 1928 to form a Taiwan Federation of Labor claiming a total membership of about 6,000. The efforts of these groups to present their claims for improved working conditions, however, were met by sharp repressive measures on the part of both government and private employers. During the thirties, as Japanese war needs grew, and as the possibility that Formosan sympathies for the Chinese would lead the local organizations to sponsor anti-Japanese political activities, the imperial authorities became exceedingly strict in their regimentation of labor, not only by direct regulation but also through support for

5. *Ibid.,* p. 49.

employers' associations. The National Mobilization Act of 1939 gave the government full authority to recruit and distribute the labor force.

After an initial period of confusion and lack of clarity regarding labor policy, the Kuomintang government has encouraged the formation of new trade unions. In the light of former conditions inside the trade unions of Shanghai, however, it appears probable that these new Formosan labor organizations will be used primarily to carry out Nationalist policy among the workers rather than to press the demands of labor on employers, public or private.

CHAPTER TEN

The Soup or the Medicine

Summing up the foregoing, is it possible to arrive at any conclusions as to how the position of the Formosan people has changed under five years of Nationalist Chinese rule?

Formosan leaders in exile maintain that conditions remain exceedingly oppressive but that the Taiwanese at home have learned from bitter experience not to give voice to their discontent. Nationalist spokesmen, on the contrary, assert that conditions have greatly improved after the unavoidable dislocations of the war-time and immediate post-war period. One of the most specific and measured statements of the improvement in the situation is given by Dr. Han. It is worth quoting in full:

The year 1937 is usually considered the peak year of Japanese rule in Taiwan. Take local income as a more reliable criterion. How does 1950, say, compare with 1937? According to a statement used by the Provincial Government, the net national income of 1937, in terms of old Taiwan dollars [yen] at 1937 value, was 724,097,359, while the figure for 1949 was 774,944,154 and for 1950 the estimate was 836,558,084. This figure is calculated "at factor cost," and represents the combined total of "domestic, net, national output" with "net income from abroad." The latter, it should be pointed out, includes at the present moment economic assistance from the Economic Cooperation Administration. It should also be pointed out that there has been a big increase in population from 5,600,042 in 1937 to 7,647,703 at present, which affects the amount of income per capita the other way. Therefore, although the net national income is estimated to be larger, income per capita may be 19 dollars less, that is, 110 as against 129. It should be remembered, of course, that, after all, 1937 was a peaceful year, the peak of 42 years of continuous rule, and Taiwan has now been only five years under the Nationalists. Again, Taiwan is still at war, with a considerable part of its efforts diverted to the defense of the island instead of for production and reconstruction.

A comparison of the national income should perhaps be paralleled with a comparison of the financial burden borne by the people. Again, according to the Provincial Government authorities, expenditures for 1950 were NT$1,797,000,000, about $205,178,910 in old Taiwan dollars of 1937 value. Divided by the total population, it comes to about 27 dollars per capita, which means 24.53 per cent of the income per capita of 110 dollars. In 1937, Government expenditures amounted to $218,635,469, or 30 dollars per capita, 30.19 per cent of the income per capita of 129 dollars then. The present financial burden on the people is therefore lighter.[1]

It is not possible to present here a careful evaluation of these figures, although the conversion of 1950 currencies to 1937 values should be taken with the greatest caution. Moreover, in comparing the cost of government it would be relevant to ask how much of the expenditure in each case contributed directly to the improvement of the lot of the population and how much was drained off into economically unproductive uses, such as military preparations. Dr. Han does concede that "confronted with hard times, present difficulties always loom larger than they were in the past. So one hears grumblings about hardships, insufficient income and the high cost of living." [2]

1. Han Lih-wu, *Taiwan Today* (Taipei, Hwa Kuo Publishing Co., 1951), pp. 53-54.
2. *Ibid.*, p. 55.

It is appropriate at this point, however, to say a few words about two points that Han raises: the increase of the population and the extent of ECA assistance.

The growth of the Formosan population has indeed been spectacular. There were about 3 million residents in 1905 when the first census was taken. By 1939 there were 5.9 million, of whom a little over 300,000 were Japanese. The aboriginal population numbered about 150,000 and has remained relatively constant. There were about 50,000 mainland Chinese resident on the island before the war. Since the war the Japanese have been repatriated and about 1.5-2.0 million mainland Chinese entered the island plus 50,000 repatriated Formosans, causing a population increase of 20 per cent. The official Chinese census report shows the island's population in January 1951 as 7.56 million but there is no analysis to show the number of native residents as compared with recent immigrants.[3]

A study of birth and death rates, however, suggests the scale of the increase which Taiwan faces. The birth rate has continued relatively constant at more than 40 per thousand up to the present time, showing even a tendency to increase. Meanwhile the death rate has declined from 33 per thousand in 1906–1909 to 20 in 1930–37, 17.50 in 1942, and, according to Han, only 12.62 per thousand in 1949. The infant mortality rate declined from 155.4 per thousand in 1934 to 77.6 in 1948, 47.9 in 1949 and 11.35 in 1950. With a crude rate of natural increase of more than 27 per thousand, or a total annual increase for the island of about 300,000, the prospects for serious overpopulation of the island within a generation are acute indeed. Dr. Yen Chun-hwei, director of the Taiwan health department, in July 1951, predicted a possible doubling of the island's

3. Chinese News Service, Press Release, March 20, 1951, p. 3.

population in thirty years.[4] Han notes that "early warnings have already been sounded for a program of birth control," but there does not as yet appear to have been any serious effort in this direction.[5] On the contrary, in accordance with the doctrines of Sun Yat-sen, the Nationalist Government seems to derive satisfaction from the prospect of rapid population growth on the ground that it will increase the manpower and therefore the potential strength of the regime for an attempt to regain control of the mainland.

The contribution of the ECA to the economy of Formosa has already been discussed. Curtailment of such aid would have a devastating impact on the island's outlook. Indeed, it may safely be said that only substantial increases in the rate of such assistance could really put Taiwan's economy on a stable basis. Whether or not such assistance can be effectively used for the strengthening of the island's defenses and production, however, will be determined in large part by the thoroughness and sincerity with which the regime carries out its projected reforms.

In any event the Nationalist Government on Formosa has a long road to travel before it can create the basis for a return to the mainland. A. T. Steele, a veteran observer of the Far Eastern scene, wrote in the New York *Herald Tribune*[6] after a visit to the island that the Nationalists were militarily, politically and ideologically unprepared for the return, no matter how much they looked forward to that hypothetical event. Pointing out that millions of Chinese accepted the Communist rule because they be-

4. *Ibid.,* July 10, 1951, p. 2.
5. Han Lih-wu, *op. cit.,* p. 53. See also *Public Health and Demography in the Far East,* by Marshall Balfour, Roger Evans, Frank Notestein and Irene Taeuber (Rockefeller Foundation, 1950), pp. 55-59.
6. May 3, 1951.

lieved it to be the lesser of two evils, Steele went on to observe that many had since become disillusioned and were looking for the emergence of new leadership. "Doubtless Chiang Kai-shek still has a large following in China," Steele continued, "and there are many who would welcome him back; but that initial enthusiasm would quickly turn to bitterness if it became evident that all the Nationalists had to offer was the same old package with a cleaner wrapping." Noting the important changes which the Nationalists had carried out, Mr. Steele stated that they had been inadequate to revive Chinese faith in Kuomintang leadership. Many observers, he said, epitomized the Formosan situation in the words of an old Chinese saying, "They have changed the soup, but they haven't changed the medicine." The future role of Formosa in Chinese history may be determined in large part by the question whether the United States, working through Chiang or through some new emergent Chinese leadership, can find a way to change the medicine as well as the soup.

Message of Chiang Kai-shek

Excerpts from message of President Chiang Kai-shek on the 39th anniversary of the Republic of China, October 10, 1950.
Source: Chinese News Service, New York, October 10, 1950.

Taiwan, the present seat of the National Government, has become a beacon light in darkness with its military reorganization, political readjustment, economic stabilization, enforcement of local self-government and introduction of social legislation. Taiwan has given bright hopes to our countrymen on the mainland. These hopes of the people will serve as a severe blow to the Russian aggressor. Let me report to you, my fellow countrymen, on the latest conditions in Taiwan.

When the Government ordered its troops to evacuate from Hainan Island and the Chusan Archipelago last April and May, I told my compatriots on the mainland that the fundamental policy of the Government could be summarized into these words: "First, concentrate all armed strength; second, safeguard Taiwan; third, rescue our compatriots on the mainland, and fourth, rejuvenate the Chinese Republic." With the concentration of our armed forces in Taiwan, this island no longer has the danger of being conquered. Its economic strength is another guarantee to our victory against Communist aggression. We must realize that Taiwan, though small in size, is economically several times stronger than any of the big and rich provinces on the mainland. As far as economic power is concerned, Taiwan is in fact equivalent to any five provinces either in the southeast or in the southwest. This is not only real strength in our anti-Communist war, but also a foundation for national revival.

We strongly believe that only a politically democratic and economically stable Taiwan can serve as our base of recovery. It is the vanguard of the anti-aggression front in Asia, and is bound to have its place in the anti-Communist front of the world. It has also contributed greatly to the security of the Pacific regions and to the peace of the world. Our conviction is firm and our work will be always to advance no matter what happens in other parts of the world. We believe that our future is bright and traitors— the Chinese Communists—and the Russian aggressor will eventually be crushed.

We are prepared to launch a counter-offensive to revenge for the entire people. Mao Tze-tung and Chu Teh, fully aware of this, cannot make any move without considering the forthcoming counter-offensive to which I am sure the people on the mainland give full support and response. Tell Mao and Chu: "If you continue your tyranny you will pay the debt with your own life and blood. Then it will be too late." . . .

Our compatriots on the mainland are groaning under starvation and terror. They cannot tolerate being made tools of Soviet imperialism and wage war against the Democracies. In order to sell our territory and sovereignty and life and property of our people to Soviet Russia, Mao Tze-tung and Chu Teh made use of all sorts of publicity aiming at destroying our racial consciousness and nationalism. Their shameless publicity and cruel class struggle and liquidation will only strengthen [the] national consciousness of our people in their struggle for freedom and survival. Such a spiritual force is many times greater than that of war against Japan. Thus, in our anti-Communist struggle, the spiritual force surpasses the material one.

The political position of Taiwan plays a far more important role than its military position. We are firmly convinced that the decisive factor of a war for independence and freedom lies in an independent and free spirit and that an independent and free government is the foundation for the construction of an independent and free nation. We will do our best and exert our utmost for national resurgence. We should not only defend Taiwan but also construct it as a model of the whole country. We should strengthen the political position of Taiwan and concentrate the spiritual force of the Chinese race so as to lay a foundation for the counter-offensive on the mainland. It is our firm conviction that the free will of the 450 million people concentrated under the banner of Blue Sky and White Sun is a guarantee for the success and triumph of national salvation and reconstruction in our anti-Communist struggle.

The nation of China has become a slaughterhouse of traitors. Mao Tze-tung and Chu Teh and our people will be converted into slaves of the Russian imperialist who demands puppets Mao Tze-tung and Chu Teh to supply blood and sweat of our people as capital for her war of attrition for the conquest of the world. We are certain that our compatriots on the mainland will have to choose between death and resistance under the tyrannical oppression of Mao Tze-tung and Chu Teh. It is my hope that our people will for the time being be patient. The Government will not let you die in starvation and terror. The

Government will come to your rescue. Thus, we take "construction of Taiwan" and "counter-offensive upon the mainland" as slogans on the Double Tenth Anniversary of this year. It is my strong belief that with concerted efforts of our 450 million people we will certainly crush Mao Tze-tung and Chu Teh and drive out the Russian imperialist from our territory.

Report by Chen Cheng

*Excerpts from report by Premier Chen Cheng to the Legislative
Yuan in Taipei, October 3, 1950.*
Source: Chinese News Service, New York, October 11, 1950.

Six months ago, the situation was extremely serious. Militarily speaking, we held only one important point on the mainland, namely, Sichang. The Communists might at any time extend their military adventures to Taiwan. Politically, as the Central Government had just moved to this island, fear and uneasiness reigned among the people. Danger also existed in our financial and economic fields. While on the one hand government revenue decreased sharply as a result of the loss of the mainland, expenses soared as more troops and refugees had arrived on this island. I felt then my responsibility was particularly heavy.

In my report to you on my administrative policy on March 31, I said, "We must concentrate all our efforts to defend Taiwan and prepare for a counter-offensive on the mainland. This is the main task of the Government at the present moment. All foreign and internal affairs must aim at attaining this objective by careful planning and speedy execution." Based upon this, we decided that in order to win sympathy and support from friendly nations, we must first of all reform our internal administration. In the military field, we must organize a smaller but better army. In the political field, social stability must be achieved and measures for local self-government in Taiwan must be enforced. Financially, we must observe a policy of retrenchment and at the same time endeavor to increase production and to develop national economy. All this was aimed at stabilizing the then existing situation.

The following is a brief report of the measures taken by the Executive Yuan in the past six months:

I. MILITARY AFFAIRS

(1) *Defense of Taiwan.* Since the fall of the mainland, the Communists have been attempting to take Taiwan by war of attrition. They had, therefore, made 11 offensives against Hainan Island and massed more than 200,000 troops for an assault on the Chusan archipelago. Fully aware of the Communists' tactics, the Government voluntarily withdrew from Hainan in April and from Chusan in May. The armed forces were thus further concentrated for the defense of Taiwan. The evacuated units could also receive further training.

(2) *Smaller but Finer Army.* To match the nation's financial resources and actual needs, the Government reorganized all armed units and agencies evacuated to Taiwan and those originally stationed in Taiwan and Kinmen (Quemoy). During the past six months, six armies, 24 divisions, two fort commands, the Chusan defense headquarters, and the Central China, Southwest and Southeast Commands, together with their subsidiary organs, were disbanded, totalling 89 units. More than 150,000 persons were discharged from the three armed forces. The remaining units have all undergone regrouping and their training has been further invigorated. The pay of the troops has been increased, and farms have been started by the

army units for their own benefit. Marked improvements in the fighting strength, discipline and morale of the armed forces can be observed. The recent victory on Tai-tan, an island near Kinmen, in which two companies of Government forces annihilated two battalions of Communist troops, is a proof of the increased fighting prowess of the Government army.

(3) *Anti-Communist Guerillas on the Mainland.* Up to the end of August, 1950, anti-communist units on the mainland maintaining contact with the Government totalled more than 1,600,000 men. Their composition is as follows: (a) those organized by officers of the National Army—about 35 per cent; (b) those organized by local militia units—about 20 per cent; (c) those organized by the people's organizations or by local leaders—about 25 per cent; (d) those organized by the border people (such as the Miaos, Yaos, and Lolos)—about five per cent; and (e) defected local Communist bands—about 15 per cent. They scatter all over the mainland and the islands off the southeastern coast. They have fought over 1,800 battles, big and small in scale, with the Communists. During these encounters, the Communists suffered more than 300,000 casualties. The Government is sending more personnel to the mainland to establish closer contact with the guerillas. . . .

II. FOREIGN AFFAIRS

. . . (6) *The Problem of Taiwan.* The United States is continuing to give economic assistance to Taiwan. The assistance given by the Seventh Fleet of the United States for the defense of Taiwan is based upon our consent and cooperation. In accordance with the Cairo Declaration and the Potsdam Proclamation, Taiwan returned to our rule after the surrender of Japan. For five years, all the people support the Government and no dissenting voice has ever been raised by any country of the world. It is our fundamental stand that there is no necessity of discussing Taiwan's legal status by the United Nations. In spite of the fact that the United States has decided to present this question to the General Assembly of the United Nations, we will continue to deal with it on the basis of our fundamental stand. . . .

III. DOMESTIC AFFAIRS

(1) *Local Self-Rule.* For the realization of the Three People's Principles and the establishment of a sound democratic government, all the *hsiens* (counties) and municipalities in Taiwan have been permitted to set up their own local governments earlier than scheduled. Beginning from April, the Executive Yuan has approved a set of General Rules for *Hsien* and Municipal Self-Government and its related regulations, and has decided that the program be carried out within a specified time in different parts of the island. A month ago, a Cabinet meeting approved the Program for the Readjustment of the *Hsien* and Municipal Administration of Taiwan which divides the province into sixteen *hsiens* and five municipalities. Through this readjustment, the area, population and wealth of each administrative unit have been more equally balanced, thus facilitating the earlier realization of local self-rule. The election of *hsien* and municipal councils as well as *hsien* magistrates and mayors and the readjustment of *hsien* and municipal administration are now in full swing and are expected to be accomplished within the shortest possible time.

(2) *Strengthening of Local Security.* The Chinese Communists have declared time and again that to attack Taiwan, a political invasion is more important than military action. What they mean is chiefly infiltration by Commu-

nist agents into this island to undermine both army and
civilian morale and to ruin by underhand means its social,
financial and economic structure. For this reason, the elimination of Communist agents has become one of the most
important tasks in the maintenance of security.

From January to July this year, security authorities in
Taiwan handled a total of more than 300 cases involving
more than 1,000 persons connected with Communist underground activities. These included the exposure of secret organizations of the Central Bureau, East China Bureau and South China Bureau of the Chinese Communists
and the spy-ring of the Soviet espionage system. In May
the Government demanded the surrender of all Communist agents in Taiwan, promising them freedom from arrest and the privilege to retain their present jobs provided
they quit their organization. Up to this date, more than
400 Communist agents have given themselves up. It can
be said that most, if not all, of the Communist organizations in Taiwan have been uncovered.

Aside from espionage, the security authorities have also
handled more than 1,000 criminal cases involving an up-
wards of 2,000 outlaws. No less than 20,000 stragglers have
been rounded up. Some of them were sent, according to
their own wish, back to the armed forces, some were given
relief, while the rest were being trained and taught ways
to make a decent living.

To uphold human rights and liberty, the Executive
Yuan specially designed a warrant of arrest and instructed
all law-enforcing bodies that no civilians subject to arrest
be taken into custody by persons other than the police. If
a warrant is issued to arrest military personnel, the organ
making the arrest must be the military police.

Communist agents under detention are now being
taught to reform themselves in accordance with a set of

measures based on the Regulations for the Elimination of Communist Agents.

(3) *Improvements in Education.* In the past six months, the Government has concentrated its efforts in helping intellectuals of the younger generation to acquire a clearer understanding of the Three People's Principles and the significance of our war against Communist aggression. Instructions were given by the Ministry of Education to all colleges and higher institutions of learning that the Three People's Principles be included in their curricula beginning from this semester. At the same time, lecture hours for courses in history, geography and social sciences are to be increased. More than 70 textbooks for primary and high school students have been revised to include more materials connected with our war effort. Social education and overseas Chinese education were also improved along this line.

Persons who formerly worked in the educational and cultural fields on the mainland and who have come to Taiwan and remain loyal to the Government were provided with proper work. Middle schools and colleges were instructed to expand their classes for students from the mainland. These students, it may be added, were encouraged to join the army, to engage in war work, or to work in productive enterprises.

For students abroad, the Government has not only been seeking means to guide them in their learning, but also promulgated a set of regulations to enable them to return and work for their motherland.

More than 4,000 graduates from middle schools and colleges in Taiwan last summer have undergone special training by the Taiwan Provincial Government and have been provided with proper work according to their abilities and wishes.

(4) *Readjustment of Government Organizations.* The repeated removals of the seat of the Government in the past year have caused a looseness of organization and spirit among the different government organs and that called for immediate readjustment to meet practical needs. Four guiding principles for such readjustment have been decided upon and promulgated by the Executive Yuan. They are: (a) All unnecessary organizations should be abolished, (b) all overlapping organizations should be amalgamated, (c) organizations handling work of a similar nature and organizations without proper control or supervision should be placed under the jurisdiction of proper authorities, and (d) the staff members of each organization must not exceed the actual number of persons needed. Based on these principles, a total of 82 organizations, including those directly under the Executive Yuan and those under the various ministries, has either been abolished or amalgamated. The number of staff members discharged totalled 4,940. Those discharged are now under proper training for re-employment.

The total number of working staff in the Executive Yuan and its various ministries has been cut down to 874 persons, representing only one-ninth of the original staff.

IV. FINANCIAL AND ECONOMIC AFFAIRS

(1) *Realization of a Balanced Budget.* The loss of the mainland to the Communists last year resulted in a drastic cut of government income although government expenditures remained stupendous. The monthly budgetary deficit before the National Government moved to Taiwan had averaged as much as 90% of the total budget. After the Government moved to Taipeh, steps were taken to retrench and develop sources of revenue, and it was due

to this double-phased policy that a balanced budget is now in sight.

In the last six months the Government neither relied on the printing press nor on the introduction of new taxes to meet its financial needs. The sharp decrease in deficit in each subsequent month and the prospect of attaining a balanced budget in the near future were due to the following three factors:

1. Increase in production, thus adding to economic stability.

2. Readjustment of the taxation system which resulted in an increase of revenue.

3. Adoption of a policy of retrenchment which has drastically cut down the expenditure.

The results of the above-mentioned policy of readjusting the taxation system and retrenchment can be best shown in the following items:

(a) *Income:*
    1. Customs revenue. With the enforcement of a set of readjustment measures, customs revenue has been on the increase. For example, the customs revenue last July registered an increase of 16 times as compared with the same period last year.
    2. Income from direct taxes and commodity taxes, and from monopoly sales of wine and tobacco has greatly increased.
    3. Land tax and land value tax. Up to the end of July, land tax collected during the present year has reached 93.95% of the total collected last year. Land value tax collected up to the end of same period has reached 84.93% of the total yearly income collected last year.

(b) *Expenditure:*

1. More than 150,000 persons in the armed forces were dismissed in accordance with the policy of organizing a small but finer army.
2. The abolishment and amalgamation of military and administrative organizations, and the retrenchment of their expenditures are also important factors.
3. The appropriation of any sum of money outside the budget requires the scrutiny by a special committee. All unnecessary or non-essential items are to be cut.

In the past six months, a strict enforcement of the budgetary system has been carried out in order to overcome the financial crisis and to attain a balanced budget. Even an item of the smallest amount of money, if unnecessary, was cut. It was through mutual understanding and the cooperation between the Government and its various branches that our financial situation has been greatly improved. The difficulties, however, still exist. To remove them we need a further increase of production and retrenchment of expenditures as well as continued understanding and cooperation from all quarters concerned.

(2) *Readjustment of the Government Enterprises.* In the last few years some of the Government enterprises have wasted public funds and suffered from mismanagement. They have not only become the target of public censure but also adversely affected the national economy and increased the financial burden of the country. An immediate improvement of the condition was in order. In June last the Executive Yuan announced a program for the improvement of the Government enterprises by making a selection of those that should be retained from those

that should be abolished according to the nature of their business and their necessity. Among those that were to be retained a number of changes was made. Starting with the reelection of the board of directors and the enlargement of their powers, they had defined for them the scope of their business and the prospect of present and future expansion. Care was taken to cut down the payroll and expenses. Up to the end of August, the number of persons dropped from the payroll totalled 847. At the present time, the different enterprises are carrying out their program step by step.

As regards the Government communication services, the respective ministries in charge are paying close attention to scientific management by introducing strict division of labor, strengthening the training in cooperation, studying the work to be done, to remuneration according to efficiency, abolition of all bad habits, and the establishment of industrial and professional tradition among the workers. In the past six months Government communication services, including the postal administration, telegraphic communication, railways, highways, and civil aviation, have made improvements according to these principles and gained excellent results. For example, the postal service had until quite recently suffered deficits. But after the recent improvement it made a profit of NT$30,000 in May. In June this profit increased to more than NT$560,-000. In August it reached NT$700,000.

(3) *Development of National Economy*. Our economic policy is aimed at the improvement of the people's economy and the financing of the war by increasing production. In agriculture our objective is to increase food production. Next we aim at the increase in production of special exportable products. In industry, we emphasize on the increase of production in fertilizers, textiles, and other

military and civilian necessities. In mining, attention is
paid to improving the quality of coal and mineral products to facilitate the export of these articles. We further
pay attention to increasing the productive capacity in the
gold and copper mines. At the same time we give assistance to private enterprises that are concerned with improving the livelihood of the people. In order to assist in
the productive enterprises of agriculture, industry, and
mining in Taiwan, we specially approved in July the increase of NT$50,000,000 in note-issue by the Bank of Tai-
wan for the specific purpose of purchasing agricultural,
industrial, and mining products so as to facilitate the flow
of capital and raise production.

In the direction of water conservancy, hydraulic power,
railways, and highways, we have either used our own
means or utilized American aid for their construction.

As regards the people's living standards, we note a
marked improvement in the livelihood of the farmers
since the introduction of the 37.5% rent schedule for the
farm lands. Hereafter we shall continue to enforce our
policy of reducing rent and pay attention to the improvement of the livelihood of laborers, fishermen, and salt pro-
ducers and the betterment of the welfare of the mountain
tribes.

(4) *Expansion of Foreign Trade.* In order to effect a
balance in the imports and exports we should pay attention to the expansion of foreign trade. Recently we con-
cluded on the basis of equality and reciprocity, a trade
agreement with Japan, which consisted of three parts,
namely, the Trade Agreement, the Financial Agreement relating to Trade, and the Program for Trade, effective from
July of this year to the end of next June. It is estimated
that the amount of trade involved will come to a total of
US$100,000,000. Under the agreement Taiwan is to export

to Japan sugar, rice, bananas, pineapples, salt, hemp, and wood pulp. Japan is to export to Taiwan fertilizers, flour, textiles, rayon, chemicals, railway sleepers, newsprints, steel and iron, and machinery. From now on we shall work for the synchronization of the different productive departments with a view to improving their management and raising the level of their techniques. This will have the effect of facilitating trade by simultaneously raising the quality and lowering the cost of production and also by the simplification of the manufacturing processes. We are also planning to expand our trade relations with other countries to expedite the improvement of the people's economy.

(5) *Rationing.* To give security to the livelihood of the government employees, we announced in July a readjustment in the treatment of the government employees, of which the following points are noteworthy:

(a) Rationing for the government employees to maintain for them a subsistence level regardless of the fluctuations in prices;

(b) Raising the pay of the technicians and teachers to encourage production and expedite reconstruction;

(c) Improving the welfare of the government employees. Under this stipulation a government employee is, in the event of marriage, bereavement, medical treatment, calamity, and education of the children, entitled to a subsidy of one to three months of his entire salary payable at once.

The foregoing schedule for the readjustment of treatment of the government employees has been enforced from August. On the theoretical side, it is based on Dr. Sun's Principle of the People's livelihood which aims at the ideal of securing a rational sharing of wealth and equalization of benefits on the part of the populace. On the practical side it takes into account the present and future fiscal and economic difficulties in trying to give to the government employees a degree of security. From now on we shall make improvements step by step as the financial and economic condition improves.

The foregoing is a brief report on the administrative measures taken during the past six months. In reviewing them, I feel that I have fallen far short of the expectations which both you and the people cherish toward me, for our work has been more negative than positive, and has been more to meet the changing situation than constructive. The administrative policy of the current year lays particular stress upon "the defense of Taiwan and preparation for a counter-offensive on the mainland." In the future we should go a step further by making "the construction of Taiwan and the counter-offensive on the mainland" our chief purpose. . . .

So far as the counter-offensive on the mainland is concerned, we have done some preparatory work during the past six months. We can roughly divide this into three stages—before the counter-offensive, during the counter-offensive, and after the counter-offensive.

(1) *Before the Counter-Offensive:* Emphasis is laid upon the development of the anti-Communist forces and the establishment of the anti-Communist administrations in the Communist-controlled areas. During the past six months, the Government has been striving in this direction. From now on, we shall try to widen the scope and redouble our efforts. We guarantee that all the anti-Communist forces within the Communist-controlled areas will receive our fullest support and recognition. We also encourage all the people in the rear who are loyal to the Government to go back to the mainland to engage themselves in the anti-Communist struggle.

(2) *During the Counter-Offensive:* Stress will be laid

upon the coordination between the military and administrative organizations as well as between them and the anti-Communist forces in the Communist-controlled areas.

(3) *After the Offensive:* Attention will be paid to the reforms and reconstruction in political, economic, educational and cultural fields so as to complete the construction of a modern state.

The guiding administrative principle for the next year is being drafted with the construction of Taiwan and the counter-offensive on the mainland as the center of our endeavor. Although we divide the task into three stages, the various programs for these three stages should all be planned before the launching of the counter-offensive. These programs will be mapped out in accordance with the teachings of Dr. Sun Yat-sen and the provisions of the Constitution. We are setting up a Planning Committee in the Executive Yuan so that we can work together to carry out our plans.

Ladies and Gentlemen. It is my opinion that we passed the real perilous period last year. Our present difficulties lie in the financial and economic fields. To sustain the prolonged anti-Communist struggle and at the same time to improve the living conditions of the people, the only way open to us is to exert our utmost in increasing production and in developing the national economy so as to raise the national income. Therefore, to construct Taiwan, we must make the development of national economy the center of all activities.

The present international situation is highly complicated. We have to be very careful in dealing with it. However, the sentiments of our people need not fluctuate with the changing international situation. We should do the best we can. When the international situation is favorable to us, we should not slacken our efforts. If the international situation is unfavorable, we should all the more work hard and seek self-help. Only by helping ourselves can we win the help of others. Only by improvements in internal affairs can we talk about foreign relations. The hearts of the people on the mainland have not been lost. Hundreds and thousands of our compatriots are engaged in the life-and-death struggle against the Communists in the Communist-controlled areas. In Taiwan the eight million people and soldiers have consolidated themselves into one unit. They swear to recover the lost territories and exert themselves for the reconstruction of our country. So long as our people can unite themselves and so long as the Government can direct all its efforts toward securing the well-being of the people, I believe all the difficulties can be overcome and our future will be bright.

Han Lih-wu, *Taiwan Today*

Excerpts from Han Lih-wu, Taiwan Today *(Taipei, Taiwan, 1951), pp. 3-25.*

As has been stated, due credit should be given the Japanese for their achievements during their occupation of Taiwan. A general foundation had been well laid in local economy, in elementary education, in public utilities and in law and order. Allowing for some inequality of treatment, life was regulated, stable and fair. However, Taiwan suffered heavily in World War II. It was squeezed hard for contributions to the Japanese war effort. Industries shrank, agriculture was crippled and the whole economy disrupted. There were devastating bombings by Allied forces which caused extensive damage and destruction. On top of all this, there was negligence, pilferage, and all kinds and manner of losses, some not unintentional, before and at the turn-over.

Taiwan was at its low ebb when returned to the Chinese national fold. The production of the most important staple food, rice, sank to about 45% of its peak production in 1938. It fell short by a quarter of the island's minimum need, not to say anything for export. Electric power dropped to 16% of its peak capacity of 1943. The biggest industry, sugar, fell to 8% of its highest production in 1940. Such examples could be multiplied in all directions.

There was yet another difficulty that confronted the Chinese take-over and which was even more serious than material damage and destruction. The Japanese had ruled Taiwan as a colony. The machinery of government was firmly in their hands. Local people were not intended to be other than the docile governed. Even during the war, when the demand on Japanese manpower was high, local people were scarcely admitted to important positions. In the first class service under the Governor, there was only one local man out of a total of 109. Of the second class of 2,226, only 7% were local men. It can, therefore, be easily realized what a great problem it was to find enough trained personnel to fill the gap left by the Japanese withdrawal. This was aggravated by the fact that the Chinese government was faced with the pressing need of taking over vast territories on the mainland.

From the beginning, however, special consideration was given Taiwan by the Chinese National Government. Prevailing practices were allowed to continue without forced conformity to national regulations. Taiwan was permitted to have a separate currency. Revenue produced in Taiwan, even if normally classifiable as national revenue, was used locally. While the National Government was not in a position to subsidize Taiwan, the island province received help in the form of UNRRA supplies and surplus goods purchased from the United States.

Then, local men were appointed to important positions hitherto barred to them. In the short space of six months, the provisional Provincial Assembly and city councils were elected and convened. At the end of the first year, regulations were promulgated mapping out a three-year program for the promotion of self-government.

But to govern Taiwan well was, as it must be, a tremendous undertaking. Shortage of trained personnel and
lack of sufficient experience and understanding which
came with years of servitude, were necessarily handicaps.
While the Government was full of good intentions and
honest purposes, there were bound to be petty opportun-
ists and unscrupulous politicians. There was one unfortu-
nate incident on February 28, 1947, which resulted in dis-
turbances and riots. . . .

Fortunately, the confusion and turmoil on the mainland did not directly affect the island. It carried on unin-
terruptedly, thanks to its geographical location. In spite of
the many shortcomings and limitations, material and
otherwise, Taiwan was able to make good progress and
forged ahead in all directions. The February 28, 1947, incident has taught both the local Chinese and mainland
Chinese an effective and good lesson. Furthermore, in view
of the deplorable condition on the mainland before and
after the Communist occupation, the Government and
people in Taiwan worked harder to make a better show
on the island.

It is now five years since Taiwan became part of China
again, and five years is not a long time. Nor were they
particularly good or propitious years for China. Yet Taiwan, under Nationalist China, is making a quick recovery, not only in comparison to the mainland, but even
with other war affected areas in the Far East. Factual accounts will bear out this claim.

Generally speaking, compared with conditions at the
time of the take-over, steady progress has been registered
in every field. In some respects, the present already equals
and may well exceed that of the best years under Japanese
rule, as for instance in rice production. In electric power,
the peak production under the Japanese has been sur-

passed. In education, not only has the number of schools and students of all grades been considerably increased, but the work now done is also of a broader nature than was possible under colonial rule.

In other respects, the present still lags far behind the Japanese record, notably in the production of sugar. Afforestation has not been kept up. Municipal services leave much to be desired. All in all, more money and labor will have to be put into the reconstruction of Taiwan. It will also need the stimulus of ready markets which Taiwan would have enjoyed if the mainland had not been occupied by the Communists.

Nevertheless, what has been achieved since October 25, 1945, when Taiwan was formally taken over, is certainly not an unworthy record. It speaks rather well of the National Government and is much to its credit. In a significant way, it shows a break from what has happened on the mainland. The strife and confusion rampant in the recent political scene on the mainland are not reflected in Taiwan. As *Time* magazine reported in its May 22, 1950, issue, "Formosa represents the greatest irony in Asia today. Here in its last refuge, Chiang Kai-shek's Government has shed the chaos and despair of the mainland." Quoting a young diplomat, it added: "This is a situation that China has not seen in years. It is a situation in which trains run on time, the island countryside is peaceful, the currency is gold-backed and no ragged refugees or beggars on the streets, no agitators inflaming the students, no discernible great abuses of economic power or large-scale corruption." . . .

The record, moreover, points to the unmistakable purpose of working for the good of Taiwan and its people. Taiwan is no longer a colony. The fortune of Taiwan and its people is linked to that of the Chinese nation. Besides,

Taiwan has its elected provisional Provincial Assembly and its quota of legislators and supervisors in the National Government. They are naturally keeping a watchful eye on the interests of the island. Then, in the Provincial Government itself, an increasing number of local people are holding key positions, and their total number in the provincial service is about double that of men from the mainland. There is, therefore, every reason to expect a general desire to work for the progress and improvement of Taiwan.

Further, according to official pronouncements, Government policies in Taiwan are based on the Three People's Principles which were much publicized on the mainland, but, unfortunately, not actually carried out. The Three People's Principles are the principles of nationalism, democracy and livelihood, comparable in a way with Lincoln's government of the people, by the people, for the people. Nationalism is a matter of feeling, understanding and, eventually, willingness to act to uphold one's nationality. It has largely to do with history, culture and education. Normally, it should be left to develop and grow from within. Hence, the aim of the Government is to concentrate on democracy and livelihood.

One cannot, of course, expect immediate results. A couple of years have necessarily to be allowed for smooth transfer, for adjustment to new conditions, and for reconstruction. In a general way, it had been announced from the start that the overall policy in Taiwan is to put into practice the Three People's Principles. It remained, however, for General Chen Cheng to vigorously pursue his policy of "livelihood first" when in 1948 he became the island's third post-war Governor.

Taiwan is essentially agricultural. About 50% of its population are farmers. Of the farmers, 70% are tenants.

One of the curses of China's rural economy is the exorbitant rental which the tenant has to pay to the landlord. This single factor accounts more than anything else for the usually wretched and impoverished life of farmers. By careful planning, determined action and the helpful cooperation of all concerned, Governor Chen was able to effect a fundamental reform in 1949, when he tackled with success this vexatious centuries-old problem. There is, as a matter of fact, nothing novel or complicated about what he did. It was an old resolution of the Kuomintang in 1924 that there should be a general reduction of 25% on rentals payable by tenant farmers to land owners. In 1930, the National Government put into its book of statutes the provision that rentals on land should not exceed 37.5% of the principal produce therefrom. This meant a substantial reduction in most cases. In other words, what Governor Chen did was to put into practice in Taiwan a major policy decision made by the National Government on the mainland and based on the principle of livelihood.

General Chen was succeeded by Dr. Wu Kuo-chen (K. C. Wu) towards the end of 1949, while the former became later the Prime Minister. On assuming office Dr. Wu announced his central policy to be the completion of self-government for . . . Taiwan. This is, of course, the foundation of democracy, the second of the Three People's Principles. Regulations pertaining to local government were considered by the provisional Provincial Assembly and Provincial Government and promulgated by the National Government. A time-table was set for the various cities and *hsien* (counties) to elect councils and mayors or magistrates, all by popular election. There was also some readjustment in the size of the various cities and *hsien* to make them better units for local government, and four new *hsien* were created as a result. Popular elections have been proceeding according to schedule. By the end of April, 1951, all the cities and *hsien* of Taiwan will be governed by their own elected mayors and councils. The results of elections already held have been satisfactory. There were no disorders and the turnout of voters was big.

It would be a mistake to exaggerate the success achieved. In democracy, local government is only the foundation and elections are but preliminaries to local government. In the improvement of the "livelihood" of the people, the tenant question is only one problem. Reduction of rental does not solve all the problems of the tenant farmer. A great deal remains to be done. Still, it cannot be denied that the improvements made represent an important step forward. If they are only beginnings, they are auspicious beginnings, and a good start has been made in putting into practice the Three People's Principles.

Again, according to official announcements, the National Government fully intends to make Taiwan a model province. There is already a fair foundation. With fertilizers, agriculture has little worries. There is good irrigation work. With an assured market, light industries can be actively developed. The people are known for their industriousness. They are also conductive [sic] to good citizenship. In an abundant way, Taiwan has therefore the essentials for being built into a model province.

There need be little or no doubt as to the Government's sincerity or determination to direct its efforts for the fulfilment of this promise. It has failed on the mainland. It realizes its past mistakes. Taiwan is now the last stand. The Kuomintang, Dr. Sun Yat-sen's Nationalist Party that sponsored the Three People's Principles and formed the backbone of the National Government, was recently reorganized. In the new deal announced by the Reorganization Committee of the Kuomintang, there was frank admission of past failures. This realization, so the announcement said, makes the Party all the more determined to do better. It is determined to get behind the Government in effecting a new deal for Taiwan and make it a model for China's other provinces. Naturally, there is little purpose in planning a beautiful program and leaving it at that. People on the mainland will want to see what the resuscitated Government can actually do in Taiwan. Any success achieved on Taiwan will serve as an inspiration to the mainland.

It is vital for the Government to do well in Taiwan. It is not only a desirable end in itself; it is also the basis of hope for eventual return to the mainland. The Government has retreated to the island not for a permanent stay. Its two-fold aim is to protect this strategic island from being seized by the Chinese Communists and also to battle the Communists until their final overthrow.

So far so good. Taiwan is rapidly becoming an island fortress. Since the National Government established itself here toward the end of 1949, much house-cleaning and tightening of the belt have taken place. There is also a gathering momentum of effectiveness and action. The Air Force is being streamlined. The Navy is undergoing rejuvenation. The Army thrives after a much needed overhaul. The chaos, confusion and defeatism that cost the mainland are gradually being transformed into a unity of purpose, determination and confidence.

It is not claimed that conditions here now approximate the ideal. But the tide that swept the Nationalist from the mainland to Taiwan has stopped short of this island fortress. And the tide has turned. The lesson was learned at a terrific price. The birth of a new nation may yet be a very painful process. Nevertheless, a start has been made in the right direction and we are witnessing the emergence of a new Taiwan under a resurgent National Government. . . .

Herein lies the significance and importance of the National Government. It is not only the effective and accepted authority on the island of Taiwan for nearly eight million people. It is the spiritual refuge of millions upon millions of Chinese on the mainland and a beacon of faith for overseas Chinese. Should a plebiscite be freely held on the mainland, there is no doubt that the majority would repudiate the Communist rule. On the other hand, should a plebiscite be held in Taiwan, it is equally certain that the great majority will choose the National Government rather than the Communists. The population of Taiwan, not including troops and militia, stood at 7,647,703, according to a census taken in October 1950. Besides 123,431 aborigines, the rest are all of Chinese stock. They or rather their ancestors came largely from Fukien, and the local dialect is that of Amoy, in southern Fukien. From their relatives and friends in Fukien and Kwangtung, or elsewhere, or from returning traders and businessmen, they have learned to dislike and distrust communism and the Communists. Then, the hundreds of thousands of refugees, who came from the mainland, in the second great migration to the island, this time to escape communist rule, all seek freedom and independence. The National Government therefore provides at once protection for around 8,000,000 free men and hope for many times more.

The importance of Nationalist China is made apparent by comparison with other areas in Southeast Asia which may be the next targets of international communism. None of these areas has a fighting force equal to that of the National Government. Then, by general recognition, Taiwan is a place that is free from communist danger from within. There are Huks in the Philippines. There are

armed dissidents in Burma. In southern India Communists are in control of a number of localities. It is no won-
der that foreign observers report that this island enjoys
such a high degree of stability that, in a way, it seems odd
that it should face a threat of invasion from the mainland
Communists. . . .

The decision of President Truman on June 27, 1950,
ordering the United States' Seventh Fleet to protect Taiwan, as a corollary to his decision to defend Korea was, of
course, welcome. The National Government also accepted
his principle of neutralization, that is, holding up air and
naval attacks on the mainland, as a temporary measure.
But it is not the intention of the Nationalists that the defense of the island be left in American hands. They are
determined to defend it themselves. They are prepared
for it. But as the Chinese Communists are receiving increasing air, naval and military assistance from the Rus-
sians, the Nationalists are in urgent need of corresponding
help. They feel that their need should not be neglected in
the interest of the common struggle against the international Communist threat.

Assistance should be extended on the basis of cooperation, if it is to bring out the best results. It is sound policy
that any help must be based on self-help. What is the position of the National Government on this account? The
answer has been given above. It is a positive one. Their
rule of Taiwan in the last five years is largely a record of
self-help. On this basis of self-help, the Economic Cooperation Administration is giving much needed aid, and cooperation between E.C.A. and the Chinese authorities is
both close and cordial. . . . In the first place, the foundation work of Taiwan has not been neglected. Extensive
electrification and good communications plus the spread
of popular education provide a solid foundation for Tai-

wan. Under the Nationalists, they have been well kept up
and even improved upon. In the second place, there has
been all round and steady progress in production, compared with the time of the take-over from the Japanese.
Thirdly, the people of Taiwan are no longer colonial sub-
jects. They are free and equal, and are being helped on
their way to self-rule.

It is naturally a heavy burden on the island, with a
large army to support, even though the National Government brought here some gold and surplus goods purchased
from the United States. It is also true that a great deal has
been done on a rather patchy basis. But the important
thing is that the Nationalists are doing an honest job and
are doing it well. Remember also that they are in a life
and death struggle with the Communists. What would become of Taiwan if it were lost! That the Government has
been able at all to maintain a high degree of stability and
a fair standard of living is no mean achievement. To expect full-scale reconstruction would be demanding some-
thing impossible without adequate outside aid. In agriculture, some fundamental work is being done, for instance,
in organizing the farmers for their own welfare. Assistance
in the planning and financing of this project is one of the
main contributions of the Joint Commission on Rural Reconstruction, a subsidiary of the Economic Cooperation
Administration in China. In industries and communications, some long needed reconditioning and additional
equipment will be possible with E.C.A. help. But there
will be a good deal that can only be done when things
return to normal, when the iron curtain is lifted from the
mainland and when a big market is again open to this island. Then there will be prosperity for Taiwan. To this
end the National Government is dedicated. There is both
determination and confidence. As an Associated Press des-

patch from Taiwan said on May 9, 1950, "People here don't seem to know what the word 'defeat' means. Chinese man in the street . . . does not doubt that Chiang Kai-shek's sun-burnt flag will eventually replace the Chinese Red's five yellow stars on red, but he likes to guess about just when the great event will be."

Statement by General Li Tsung-jen

Statement issued to the press by Li Tsung-jen in December 1951.

. . . On Formosa, Chiang Kai-shek is repeating in many cases exactly what he did on the mainland.

a. The system of divide-and-rule has been introduced into the administration, the party and the armed forces.

b. While on the mainland the ruling group was confined to about half a dozen favorites around Chiang Kai-shek, now in Formosa, he cannot trust anybody else except his two sons. The younger son, Chiang Wei-kuo, commands the machinized forces. The elder son, Chiang Ching-kuo, controls other ground forces through his political commissars who are the real commanders in the army. The commanding generals are mere figureheads.

c. Chiang Ching-kuo is also head of the secret police. The secret police spys on the government officials, the merchants, the teachers, the students and curiously enough, the other secret police. Everybody is shadowed and no one ever feels safe.

d. Almost all civil rights are suppressed. . . . In fact, to criticize the government is a crime. The movement of the people is strictly controlled as in Soviet Russia. Chinese are not allowed to enter Formosa without special permission. People in Formosa are not allowed to leave the island without special permission and substantial contribution to the government.

e. Corruption and graft are now practiced on a smaller scale simply because the territory under Chiang Kai-shek's control is now much smaller.

Joshua Liao, *Formosa Speaks*

Author's preface to Joshua Liao, Formosa Speaks *(Hongkong, Formosan League for Re-emancipation, 1950).*

"They desire to see no territorial changes that do not accord with the freely expressed wishes of the peoples concerned," provides the Atlantic Charter formulated by President Roosevelt and Premier Churchill in 1941.

In 1943 the Cairo Conference attended by President Roosevelt, Premier Churchill, and Generalissimo Chiang Kai-shek decided to hand Formosa to China after the Japanese surrender. Such an arbitrary action was committed not in accordance with the freely expressed wishes of the Formosan inhabitants.

Historically, the Japanese in 1895 with brutal force occupied the island neither from the Manchus nor from the Chinese, neither from Chiang Kai-shek nor from Mao Tsetung, but from its rightful inhabitants. Because the Manchu Court ceded Formosa to Japan not in accordance with its inhabitants' wishes, the Formosans established the independent Formosan Republic, though subsequently driven into colonial status. The Chinese Government by its inability to help the Formosans resist the Japanese invaders must have forfeited any claim to it long ago. Today the ejected regime from China seeking shelter in Formosa is not entitled to administer the island's state affairs because its status remains undecided pending the conclusion of the peace treaty with Japan. The Cairo decision must be abrogated because it contradicts the Atlantic Charter.

Besides, the misgovernment of Formosa must have disqualified China as a trustee power. Upon the Japanese surrender in August, 1945 every Formosan hoped to have liberty, equality, and fraternity if and when reunited with China as the people of Alsace-Lorraine with France. For five years after VJ Day, however, the Chinese officials and soldiers have been preaching fraternal reunion but practised colonial reconquest and committed all kinds of political outrages. In consequence, they have lost all Formosan loyalty and enthusiasm. Nowadays the Formosans hate the Chinese as much as the Japanese. Not that they are revolting against China, but that the Chinese in Formosa as represented by the worst types of undesirables have deserted them. Having realized the futility of any further appeal for Chinese sympathy, they prefer to recover their independence lost in 1683 and 1895.

With their group-consciousness growing into Formosan Nationalism, neither Chinese-made nor Japanese-imported, the Formosan Patriots want to regain political independence through a plebiscite under neutral supervision, failing which recourse to arms will be the only alternative. For liberty and prosperity they are determined to fight on even longer than the Irish did.

What is Chiang Kai-shek, head of the Chinese Government in Formosa? In China he abused all administrative powers, arrogated all victory-merits, controlled the whole national treasury, and ignored the people's rights. When the Communists and the Democrats wanted to have peace with him, he declined their request; when the Nationalist officers and men were tired of fighting, he ordered them to the battle-front. In the end he incurred defeat after defeat, till his whole entourage was wiped out of China and has sought refuge in Formosa. In the island, though its legal status remains undecided, he has been issuing orders and enforcing decrees, commandeering provisions and conscripting labourers, like Maximilian over the Mexicans. In China one uniformed man is supported by one hundred civilians; in Japan and Germany one occupation soldier, by several hundred vanquished people; but in Formosa one refugee tyrant, by ten natives. With young and old, women and invalids, excluded, every two able-bodied Formosans have to house and feed one Chinese soldier. The "war debt" Formosa is paying China far exceeds the Japanese and the German war-reparations, indeed!

As to his henchmen and kinsmen in Formosa, their lack of public spirit caused the speedy and spectacular collapse of the Kuomintang Army and economy in China. After VJ Day they boasted of the quantities of the taken-over raw materials and finished products, trucks and boats, factories and machinery, but, grabbed or wasted them instead of utilizing them for public interests and productive purposes. And, by forcing the people to convert their gold bars and foreign currencies into the Gold Yuan half a year before they evacuated Nanking they stripped many earnest citizens naked. What was true in China has been even more true in Formosa!

Unable to bear Chinese tyranny and robbery, we, Formosan Patriots, have been for years presenting the Case of Formosa before the civilized world for judging between the Chinese wrong and the Formosan right and by all means attempting to enlist foreign sympathies and contact the United Nations, SCAP, and Governments of the Democratic World. Now that the item, "The Question of Formosa's Future Status," submitted by the US Chief Delegate, Mr. Warren Austin, to the UN General Assembly, has been placed on the agenda, the island's future status must be changed according to its natives' aspirations.

Hwang Chao-ch'in, one of the new delegates whom the KMT regime has sent to the United Nations is a Formosan but in the capacity of the Chairman of the Taiwan Provincial Council and Governor of a KMT-sponsored bank cannot represent the Formosan people. It is therefore imperative that facts and aspirations be fairly presented by a free native Formosan to the United Nations, for which the present author has written down and sent out this memorandum, "Formosa Speaks."

The civilized world must consider the present status of Formosa as undecided and the ejected Chinese regime there as ex-lex and must give the Formosans a chance to decide their future status according to the Atlantic Charter. To uphold international justice, the United Nations should see to it that Lake Success become no Munich for selling a people like chattel attached to their inhabited land. It is therefore up to the United Nations to inaugurate an international administration: (1) To take over the government units from the present regime in Formosa, (2) to disarm the Chinese troops there and employ them for labour services pending their repatriation, (3) to release all Formosans arrested on the charge of political treason (as the objective of Formosan loyalty remains also undecided), and (4) to allow free political activities of different parties in Formosa pending the holding of a plebiscite for (a) complete independence, (b) union with CCP China, and (c) retention of the KMT status quo.

Since only those who had been citizens of Formosa before VJ Day will be entitled to vote during the plebiscite held under neutral observation, we are absolutely sure an overwhelming majority of our people will vote for complete independence. They will become unhappy again if placed under any foreign rule that implies the revival of colonialism against which they have been fighting for three odd centuries. In population (over 7,000,000) and industry (throughout Asia only next to Japan) our country is comparable with the majority of the independent nations in the world; in cultural advancement (90% literacy) and social organization (well-regimented and law-abiding) our people are highly qualified to manage their own affairs and direct their future destiny. Therefore, they must have a chance to express their joint-wishes freely for independence in accordance with the principle and practice of democracy.

Bibliographical Note

In the preparation of this study I have drawn heavily on Dr. Han Lih-wu's able volume, *Taiwan Today,* published in Taipei by the Hwa Kuo Press, 1951. Other semi-official Nationalist sources used were the press releases of the Chinese News Service, published in New York, and the *China Monthly,* issued in Taiwan. A good deal of supplementary data may be obtained in the *Directory of Taiwan,* 1951, published by the China News and Publication Service, Taipei. A number of statistical and other reports are also issued by various agencies of the Nationalist Government in Chinese. In particular the quarterly report of the Bank of Taiwan was used to check some of the statistical data.

Two articles by George Kerr—"Formosa's Return to China," *Far Eastern Survey,* October 15, 1947, and "Formosa: the March Massacres," *Far Eastern Survey,* November 5, 1947—give a first-hand account of some events of the first post-war years. I have also had the privilege of consulting a manuscript by Joshua Liao, which affords an insight into the attitude of Formosan separatists on some of the political developments of the period. Some of Liao's material has already been published in a pamphlet entitled *Formosa Speaks* (Hongkong, Formosan League for Re-emancipation, 1950).

For the work of the Economic Cooperation Administration in Formosa, I have drawn on ECA's quarterly reports to Congress, and on the pamphlet entitled *U.S. Economic Assistance to Formosa*, 1 January to 31 December 1950 (ECA, 1951). Detailed information about the program and work of JCRR is also provided in a report published in Hongkong in May 1950, entitled *Joint Commission on Rural Reconstruction, General Report*, October 1, 1948 to February 15, 1950. The MSA Mission to China has recently begun to issue a monthly mimeographed bulletin entitled *Chinese-American Economic Cooperation* (Taipei, January 1952 on). It contains a wealth of information about current developments, but was received too late for use in this study.

The "China White Paper" (*United States Relations with China*, Department of State Publication 3573, Far Eastern Series 30, 1949) contains a brief account of United States policy toward Formosa to 1949 (pp. 307-310), and a detailed report on Chinese administration there (document number 169, pp. 923-938).

For general background regarding Formosa a convenient summary volume is *Formosa Today*, by Andrew J. Grajdanzev (New York, Institute of Pacific Relations, 1942). A large compilation of detailed material regarding all aspects of the island before the end of World War II is contained in the Navy Civil Affairs Handbooks, *Taiwan* and *Taiwan-Economic Supplement* (Navy Department Publications OPNAV 50E-12 and 13, 1944). A convenient, though summary, treatment of Formosan affairs is given in "L'Ile de Formose," published by the French Ministry of Finance and Economic Affairs in the series, *Notes et études documentaires*, number 1189, September 1, 1949. A recent volume combining valuable factual information with a good journalistic impression of the island is H. M. Bate, *Report from Formosa* (New York, Dutton, 1952).

For the findings of a survey trip to investigate population problems see *Public Health and Demography in the Far East* by Marshall C. Balfour, Roger F. Evans, Frank W. Notestein, and Irene B. Taeuber, published by the Rockefeller Foundation in 1950, pp. 53-60.

A characteristic exposition of the Communist point of view may be found in Alexandrov, "The Island of Taiwan (Formosa)," *Pravda*, January 13, 1951, translated in *Soviet Press Translations*, Volume 6.

Frequent, though fragmentary, accounts of developments in Formosa are contained in American newspapers, especially the *New York Times* and New York *Herald Tribune*. For the military analysis of this study, I am especially indebted to three articles by Philip Potter published in the *Baltimore Sun*, as well as to an article by Robert S. Elegant in *The Reporter*, December 25, 1951.

F. W. R.